REVIEW OF

Men Too

While sexual assault is a most violent crime and violation against an individual, child sexual assault is among the most abhorrent acts. Not only is the assault (or assaults) traumatic, but the betrayal of trust and potential long-term effects of the assault often mean that the individual has problems for many years, even for life. When one hears of child sexual assault, an initial thought might be that a young female is the victim. However, increasing numbers of media reports and accounts are revealing that males, especially young males, are victims too. Although the revealing of male sexual assault is important in dealing both with perpetrators and the conditions that enabled such assaults to occur, comparatively little is known about the experiences of male sexual assault survivors from their own perspectives. This information is important, not only to hear their accounts and stories of how they survived and cope but to gain understanding about the ongoing effects they deal with and to suggest how therapists might better help such individuals. Moreover, the author, Dr. Kelli Palfy, also states that the book is intended to help male survivors of sexual assault. While Dr. Palfy is a practicing Registered Psychologist, she had previously been a Royal Canadian Mounted Police officer who worked extensively with sexual assault victims and the pursuit of the perpetrators of the assaults. In consequence, she has a broad and extensive range of experience dealing with sexual assault survivors, both from the "front line" and from the perspective of a therapist. She also notes that initially she did not consider that there were many male sexual assault victims. Her discovery that this idea was wrong motivated her to study male sexual assault and from the perspective of the survivor. The accounts of 13 male sexual assault survivors are presented with comments and analyses.

Dr. Palfy jumps in immediately by describing Jacob's experience and makes the important point that, in many cases, assaults go unreported because of myriad reasons, including that in many contexts, the discussion of sex is taboo and there appears to be little support available to ameliorate and redress the situations that led to the assault, or tragically, the many assaults.

Good historical background is provided with excellent connections to current and recent events and scholarly literature. Similarly, clear descriptions are provided about definitions, what constitutes the identification and etiology of a pedophile, and the various methods that have been used by such individuals to "groom" potential victims by referring to actual cases beyond this study.

The accounts from the 13 participants reflect often different circumstances, outcomes, and long-term effects. Abusers range from family members and relatives to members of the community, such as teachers, coaches, and priests. The abuse is sometimes of relatively short duration and in some instances occurred over several years. The information revealed is vivid and often disturbing. Nevertheless, it must be borne in mind that these events occurred and that the accounts are from the actual survivors. The book is excellent in weaving together the accounts of the survivors, as well as explanations and clarifications by the author. Throughout the book are highlighted summaries of important information, such as how one can recognize if a child is being groomed and "was I really a victim?" More extensive discussion of such matters occurs later on in the book.

Discussions concerning why many men do not disclose, examination of the specific reasons given, and the long-term effects of sexual abuse on males are also presented. In some respects, the effects of the sexual abuse on the survivors are as disturbing as the accounts of the actual abuse with some survivors experiencing, among other things, posttraumatic stress disorder (PTSD), memory loss, suicidal thoughts, shame, and questioning their sexual identity with resulting problems forming adult romantic relationships. While some of the 13 survivors show remarkable resilience and live reasonable lives as adults, a key point made in the book is that "sexual abuse is always damaging."

That all of the survivors were receiving help is a most positive aspect of the book. While the reasons for seeking help are varied, therapy appeared to be beneficial to all. In spite of what the survivors went through, there remains a general reluctance to disclose and share experiences. Apart from fear of negative repercussions, there is a perception that it remains "culturally unacceptable for men to be victims" (p. 127). The author also addresses social and faith issues as the result of surviving sexual assault and provides extensive discussion about these matters, again with a focus on helping survivors and practitioners.

The book is not only a powerful testament of male sexual assault survivors, but it also provides an extensive and scholarly analysis of the factors contributing to male sexual assault, what can be done to help survivors, and also importantly, help to minimize incidents in future. "As a society, we need to make more room for abused boys and men to come forward. We need to advertise that we will support them, begin to have the tough conversations, and remove the stigma" (p. 166).

Men Too is an essential resource for practitioners, those who are in positions to detect sexual abuse, and for survivors who may take some solace in realizing that they are not alone and that there are some in society who will endeavor to help rather than to exploit.

George H. Buck, Ph.D.
Professor and Chair
Dept. of Educational Psychology
University of Alberta

ME ᵛN TOO

UNSPOKEN TRUTHS ABOUT MALE SEXUAL ABUSE

DR. KELLI PALFY

Peaks & Valleys Publishing
peaksandvalleyspublishing@gmail.com

ISBN: 978-1-9992925-1-5 (print)
ISBN: 978-1-9992925-0-8(ebook)

Scripture taken from the New King James Version®. Copyright © 1982 by Thomas Nelson. Used by permission. All rights reserved.

Ordering Information:
Special discounts are available on quantity purchases by corporations, associations, and others. Please contact Peaks & Valleys Publishing for more details.

This book is dedicated to
the men who shared their stories,
to those who have yet to share,
and to those who encouraged me
to write this book.

CAUTIONARY NOTE

Many of the stories in this book may be hard to read due to their graphic content. Nonetheless, they are true, neither exaggerated nor embellished for dramatic effect. They are told to convey to you what takes place in our society—to inform and educate you about male sexual abuse. If you become emotionally overwhelmed, I suggest you pause, disengage from reading this book, and take care of yourself. If you are an abuse survivor yourself, I recommend finding and working with a trained trauma therapist who specializes in sexual abuse to assist you in your healing process.

Peppered throughout the book are psychoeducational pieces (in text boxes) explaining the emotional and physiological experiences of traumatized individuals. Additional resources for further reading are listed at the back of the book. This information doesn't qualify anyone to begin treating abuse victims without professional training.

Please note the terms "offender," "perpetrator," "abuser," and "molester" are used interchangeably and are intended to mean the same thing. The word "disclose" is used to refer to the sharing of personal information, in this case the experience of confiding in or telling someone about abuse.

CONTENTS

INTRODUCING THE LIFE OF JACOB

Jacob injured his knee in his sophomore year of high school, "bent it at a right angle sideways," during football practice. His coach rushed him to the hospital where doctors told him he needed immediate surgery. They needed his father's permission to operate and requested he come to the hospital immediately.

When Jacob's father finally arrived four hours later the coach was furious. He asked why it had taken him so long to get to the hospital.

"We haven't been able to give him any pain medication," the coach stated.

His father rationalized, *"Well, I was shingling the shed, and when the shingles are running straight through you don't stop."*

"But Jacob has been sitting here in pain for hours!" the coach protested.

"He can put up with it," Jacob's father responded.

Disgusted, but trying to sidestep a further argument, the doctor asked Jacob's father to sign and consent so he could do the recommended surgery. Jacob's father refused.

The doctor pleaded with him. *"If he doesn't have the surgery, he will have problems later in life."*

"That's not my problem," he replied.

The doctor couldn't believe a father could be so callous toward his own son. He pled with him further.

"His knee is going to constantly come in and out of joint and will lock up on him. He'll be falling down stairs and by the time he's in his fifties, he'll be in pain."

"By the time he gets to 50, I'll be dead," Jacob's father declared, and denied Jacob the surgery.

Later that day Jacob's father told him that a female doctor would be coming to talk to him. He warned Jacob not to say a word to her.

Two days later, a female psychiatrist came into his room. *"The nurses heard you crying at night and I came in to speak to you about what's bothering you."* She asked Jacob several times if things were alright at home. He said nothing. He didn't trust that the psychiatrist, or anyone else, could help him. He was not aware of any children that had ever been removed from their parents' care, and he believed his parents would take revenge on him for talking. They might even kill him.

Jacob's fear was for valid reason. Throughout his youth, other professionals had good reason to suspect he was being abused (his own grandmother even witnessed him being sexually abused) yet nothing was ever done to stop it. Jacob believed the only way to escape the abuse was to survive until he was able to move out on his own. In the end he was right. No one ever came to his aid.

#MeToo is an important global movement in support of female sexual abuse survivors. Just as dialogues about women as victims of sexual abuse and harassment are needed, so are discussions about male victims of abuse. Jacob's story—and countless untold stories like his—highlight an equally important need to discuss male sexual abuse which is still widely unreported and unacknowledged. This lack of recognition is in part because the boys and men who experience it rarely come forward. They remain silent for a multitude of reasons, including their own confusion, guilt, fear, desire to protect others, and lack of understanding. Many worry that they will be perceived as "less of a man" if they disclose having been abused. Others fear they will be considered future sexual offenders.

Research conducted in the United States has shown that approximately one out of every six males is sexually assaulted before the age of 16; yet very few of these individuals disclose, pursue charges, or seek treatment.[1] The most recent Statistics Canada surveys (from 2004 and 2014) indicate that males report sexual abuse at a rate of 7 (2004) and 5 (2014) per every

1,000 men. A very small percentage of men self-report sexual assaults in this country.[2]

Who Is This Book For?

First and foremost, this book is written for male survivors of sexual abuse, many of whom still do not recognize themselves as having been victimized. Men and boys often fail to understand they've been abused for any number of reasons which I discuss in this book. My hope is that through reading the detailed stories shared in this book, other boys and men will gain a better understanding of what abuse looks like, come to recognize themselves as victims and begin to heal and recover. This book is not designed to replace therapy but to supplement healing and inspire men to both seek and accept professional help.

Second, this book is for helping professionals, as well as the friends and family of male survivors. My hope is that through increased awareness, that the helping professionals, friends and families of male victims will become better supports. If this group of people can create safer spaces to talk about male sexual abuse, and not shy away from engaging in the difficult but necessary conversations, abused boys and men will have improved access to healing. Through more open lines of communication, men will feel safer both asking for and accepting help. Whether on an individual level or a cultural level, we cannot conquer what we won't address.

The heart of this book is comprised of the stories of 13 men who were sexually abused as boys, adults, or both. I personally interviewed each of them. Using the information each disclosed, I will explain how their abuse began, how it was sustained, and how it eventually ended. I also share the reasons why many of them initially failed to see themselves as victims. As you read these heart-wrenching stories, I urge you to remember that healing *is* possible.

Who I Am and How I Came to Work with Male Survivors

You may be wondering why a female psychologist has an apparent passion for working with male sexual abuse survivors, since I am clearly not one myself. In answer to this, I will explain the process of how I developed both my awareness of, and my interest in serving, this population.

Prior to becoming a psychologist, I was a Royal Canadian Mounted Police (RCMP) officer. In 2004, I was assigned to the Integrated Child Exploitation (ICE) unit in British Columbia, where I had the opportunity to witness boys as victims of sexual abuse. The ICE unit was established after the US Postal Inspection Service noted a significant number of suspicious-looking parcels and engaged in a joint investigation with the Federal Bureau of Investigation (FBI), the Department of Homeland Security, and Immigration and Customs Enforcement. Their investigation revealed that the parcels contained pornographic images of children, which had all been purchased via credit card. Many of the credit card owners were found to be living in Canada. The RCMP responded by forming the ICE unit to both organize and disseminate the information to the appropriate detachments for follow-up investigation.

In addition to working in the ICE unit, I also worked part-time doing undercover work and was being trained to target offenders in online chat rooms. I'd pose as a potential offender who was looking to trade images, chat with someone briefly, then leave and check out a different chat room. Within seconds, the offender would find me and badger me for images. The number of skilled and persistent offenders shocked me and opened my eyes to the magnitude of the problem.

If you have seen the movie *Spotlight*, which chronicles how *The Boston Globe* exposed the Catholic Church sex abuse crisis, you may recall the scenes where the journalists experience a similar awakening. In one scene, they are in a library looking at the records of four priests accused of offending against young boys. On record, the priests were listed as either "transferred" or "on medical leave," and so were numerous others. The reporters began to suspect a massive systemic cover-up and investigated further. They identified the names of 200 more priests who were also listed as being on medical leave or transferred. The lights began to go on. The reporters suspected that these priests may also have been suspected of abusing children. As they began to investigate each name, their discovery process mirrored my own. The ICE would investigate an offender, seize their computer, and gain access to their electronic address book. This address book would then be found to contain the email addresses of other offenders whom they had likely met online and traded child pornographic images with.

In 2002, Canada passed a law stating that any Canadian who travelled abroad and engaged in sexual acts with children could be charged criminally as if they had committed the acts in Canada. Soon after, investigative files began to surface. In 2004, I became the file coordinator for the RCMP's first "sex tourism" case, which involved a now-convicted pedophile. The file began after a Canadian returned home from Colombia. He had sent a parcel containing CDs home in advance of his arrival. These disks contained evidence of crimes he had committed in Columbia, Cambodia and the Philippines. The Vancouver Airport Authority had searched this parcel and found videos of him sexually abusing children. This file became the second investigation using the newly enacted sex tourism legislation in Canada.

At the same time, the Vancouver Police Department (VPD) was in the process of laying Canada's first set of sex tourism charges against Donald Bakker, who had travelled to Cambodia and engaged in sexual relations with children. A woman he had brutally sexually assaulted in Canada had disclosed to police that Bakker had videotaped the entire assault. Police obtained search warrants, seized his video camera, and located several tapes containing images of him abusing children in Southeast Asia. While the VPD was still attempting to identify the crime scene locations, *Dateline NBC* aired a documentary exposing the problem of child sexual abuse taking place in brothels abroad. When this episode aired, an RCMP forensic scientist recognized rooms, furniture and victims that were "eerily" similar to those in Bakker's home videos. Investigators then travelled to Cambodia to complete their investigation. I met one who described having witnessed young children being sold in cages like animals, waiting to be used as sex slaves. This person was devastated. The VPD were powerless to stop the abuse since they had no legal authority in Cambodia. My heart went out to these children and to the VPD investigative team who were blocked from intervening.

SEX SLAVERY AND HUMAN TRAFFICKING

In developing countries where families have little to no food and no access to clean water, parents are often forced to "sell" one of their children as a means to provide for the rest of their children. The sale of one's child is not a malicious practice but rather an act of desperation when parents see no other means of supporting their other children. These parents are often told their child will be trained to become a nanny or be given a housekeeping job, prospects that are far more innocent than their horrific reality.

On one of my ICE training courses, I had the privilege of attending a private lecture by former pro hockey player Sheldon Kennedy. He spoke candidly about the abuse he suffered at the hands of Graham James, the former Canadian Western Hockey League coach who later went to prison for sexually abusing young men on his teams. One thing Kennedy spoke about was living a double life. He explained that on the one hand he was a professional hockey player; yet on the other he was a victim who felt the need to remain silent. He and his parents were benefitting considerably from his success, and he worried about what coming forward might do to his hockey career. He also spoke about the fact that he began using alcohol and drugs as a means of coping with the abuse.

I related to Kennedy's concept of leading a double life. Although I'd not been sexually abused, I'd experienced significant bullying and harassment (at work), and I too felt like I had lived a double life. On one hand I was a police woman with a badge and a gun, working in enviable positions for one of the top police departments in Canada. On the other hand, over the years I'd often gone home in tears because of the bullying I was experiencing. I too felt powerless to expose it lest it end my career.

Mr. Kennedy's honesty touched me profoundly and left me with the understanding that society had failed him. It also caused me to rethink things I'd questioned in the past. Prior to becoming an RCMP officer I worked as a corrections officer, and I recalled wondering why a disproportionate number of men ended up in the justice system after having "chosen" a lifestyle of crime and addiction. After Mr. Kennedy's lecture I began to recognize that maybe they hadn't chosen the lifestyle so much as succumbed to it. In 2010, I completed my master's practicum at the British Columbia Society for Male Survivors of Sexual Abuse, received further training, and came to better understand male victims of sexual abuse and the barriers they faced when considering coming forward and telling their truth.

Maintaining the Silence

The global #MeToo movement, which went viral in 2017, supports female sexual abuse survivors but rarely focuses on men as victims. Although men are encouraged to join the conversations, provide their support for the movement, and get on board and assist in stopping sexual violence against women (all good and necessary ventures), male voices as victims are still seldom heard. Sadly, this is true even among helping professionals.

In 2017, actor and former NFL player Terry Crews was among the few adult men to publicly identify himself as a #HeToo victim after disclosing that he was groped by a Hollywood executive at a party the previous year. My guess is Crews was targeted by his abuser in part because no one would suspect a "tough guy" like him would ever come forward and admit to having been victimized as an adult. I applaud him. His abuser obviously had no idea the depth of strength and courage he had.

Academic research has previously been conducted on the struggles men commonly face when considering disclosing sexual abuse. One study— appropriately titled "Deep and Almost Unbearable Suffering: Consequences of Childhood Sexual Abuse for Men's Health and Well-Being" — explored the consequences of childhood sexual abuse on the health and well-being of 14 Icelandic men, all of whom had lived with profound depression. None of the men disclosed their abuse until well into adulthood, when "they hit rock bottom and faced the choice of revealing what had happened or taking their own life."[3]

According to the study, one of the things that kept these victims silent was the myth that men who endured sexual abuse as children will become sexual offenders themselves. Each man was convinced that people would assume they were primed to begin abusing children someday. Still, despite this intense fear as well as their fear of not being believed, each chose to disclose his abuse rather than kill himself. This finding begs the question: How many abused men have chosen the alternative?

Jackson Katz, an American educator, author and cofounder of Mentors in Violence Prevention, equated childhood sexual abuse to an incubator for making violent men. He asserted that male victims sometimes feel the only way to get respect when all has been lost is through engaging in violence.

"So many of these boys who were victims grow up to deal with it the only way they know how, which is to go out and take back that which was wrongfully taken from them,"[4] Katz said.

Consequently, in Western culture, many abused boys and men encounter helping professionals, including the police, while displaying anger and engaging in destructive coping mechanisms. At this point they are seldom recognized as victims.

How Traditional Gender Biases Impact Male Victims

In Western culture males are still largely denied their right to be victims. Although people are becoming more aware that boys and men are abused, many do not understand how it happens, its frequency or the fact that it is not limited to the stereotypical scenarios of one-time encounters at summer camp or falling prey to a corrupt coach or priest. Of the research and plethora of books that discuss childhood sexual abuse, most have traditionally focused on the consequences for girls and women who have been abused by older boys and men. This focus on girls has led people to believe that the sexual abuse of boys is rare. This is not the case.

In generations past, and still today, boys are conditioned from their youth to believe that "real men" are strong, confident, resilient, self-sufficient[5] and incapable of being victims. Boys are encouraged not to cry or be dependent on others.[6] Breaching these masculine principles can leave them being viewed as less of a man. Boys are taught that real men are providers, capable of protecting themselves and others, and of course always wanting sex. Growing up, boys also are conditioned to believe that arousal is a sign of interest and intent, yet this is not always the case.

The result of this conditioning is that boys and men often disown their vulnerabilities in order to protect their masculine image. Abiding by traditional masculine gender stereotypes leaves little room for men to be victims.[7] Not surprisingly, many male victims struggle to understand that what happened to them was in fact abuse. This has to change. The American Psychological Association recently highlighted the harmful aspects of cultural masculinity, along with the biases that exist even among psychologists who work with boys and men. They have called for greater awareness of these biases and pointed to research highlighting that school-age boys still do not receive the help they need, despite being overrepresented in social, psychological, behavioral and learning problems; later in the prison and in the completed suicide population (as reflected in incarceration and suicide statistics).[8]

Because male sexual abuse violates many of Western culture's expectations regarding gender roles, when males are victimized it often causes them to doubt their own sense of masculinity.[9] To compensate for feelings of inadequacy, male victims often adopt attitudes of hyper-masculinity. They guard their secret and adopt behaviors that assert their masculinity in culturally acceptable, yet excessive ways.[10] Many become angry, since anger has traditionally been one of the few socially acceptable emotions that men are "allowed" to express.[11]

Consequently, male survivors often use destructive coping mechanisms, like drugs or alcohol to numb or distract themselves from their pain. Others cope by becoming work-a-holics, or by getting involved in weightlifting, football, hockey or other aggressive sports, where they attempt to prove their masculinity to both themselves and to others. Perhaps in no other arena are gender-based messages stronger than in organized sports, where boys are treated as pseudo-men and made to compete and prove themselves. They are given overt messages to "suck it up," "shrug it off," and "take it like a man" by coaches and fellow players who encourage them in their transition toward manhood.[12]

Paradoxically, sexual abuse is widespread in male-organized sports,[13] as evidenced in both research and in the testimonies of professional hockey players Theoren Fleury[14] and Sheldon Kennedy. In 2006, Kennedy released a book titled *Why I Didn't Say Anything: The Sheldon Kennedy Story.*[15] He disclosed that during the trial against his coach, Graham James, the police estimated that James had "molested 75 to 150 kids who were under his care during his time as a coach, manager and scout. Many of those players were great talents, but almost all of them dropped out of minor hockey before they had a chance to be drafted."

Because men have traditionally not been allowed to talk about experiences of abuse, most don't. Instead, they cope through the use of denial, sometimes with the help of alcohol or drugs. They isolate themselves and avoid intimacy. A significant number of boys and men never talk about their abuse because talking about it would place them in an extremely vulnerable position.[16] Since recovery generally involves traversing the emotional territory men are culturally encouraged to avoid, many choose to remain silent. Although they may appear to live normal lives, on the inside many are struggling with feelings of shame, confusion and self-doubt.

The Confusion of Involuntary Arousal/ Arousal Non-Concordance

In consensual sexual encounters, arousal and orgasms are desired and welcome outcomes. During abuse, they aren't. While getting an erection is a normal bodily response to penile stimulation, being involuntarily "aroused" during an assault is not indicative of willingness or enjoyment. During a sexual assault it is common for both men and women to have genital manifestations of arousal, despite the fact that they are not enjoying themselves.

Many boys and men experience a lack of control over spontaneous erections, even ejaculation, in response to anxiety-provoking stimuli. Comedic movies, for instance, often depict male teens with erections during math or gym class. Despite this awareness, abused males forget when recalling their abuse that not all erections are associated with sexual fantasy.

Instead, they recall only what they have been taught about men being able to have control over when, where and with whom they have erections. They rationalize that, although the abuse began as nonconsensual, they must have begun to enjoy it and changed their minds. They believe their perpetrator must not have forced, but rather seduced them into a state of arousal, making the act consensual. Alternatively, they believe there is something seriously wrong with them for having "enjoyed" the abuse. This is not the case.

Many are confused not only by their physical response, but also by the loving words and kind gestures of friendship offered by the perpetrator before or during their abuse. They recall feeling special, cared for, even loved. Boys who are not brutally or violently raped also are often confused because they enjoyed how it felt to ejaculate. Many feel guilty because they return to their abusers and engage in other sexual encounters. Some believe because they ejaculated, they might be attracted to men.

Although involuntary arousal is troubling for both genders, there are crucial distinctions in the way genital arousal can affect a male's ability to process it while it's happening. While some women have orgasms that are so intense they overpower and render them momentarily unconscious, others have difficulty recognizing their orgasms.[17] Since women's orgasms can be harder to detect, women can more easily ignore, deny, or minimize their physical responsiveness to trauma-induced arousal.

In contrast, because male arousal is visible to all parties, boys and men can't deny, ignore, or minimize it, even if it wasn't consensual. In addition, their offenders often use this against them as "evidence" of their pleasure and willingness to participate. This particularly confuses young boys. Ultimately, perpetrators often try to make their victims believe they liked and even invited the assault.[18] And the victims often feel as if their bodies have betrayed them.

One study estimates that approximately 20 percent of male victims ejaculate during sexual assault.[19] Researchers also cite cases where males sustained erections during assaults committed under extreme situations of distress, including at gunpoint and while being handcuffed, gagged, beaten, drugged, tied up, and threatened with castration for not performing.[20] Evidence clearly shows that men can become aroused despite a lack of consent and emotional desire.

In a 2018 TED Talk, sex educator and author Dr. Emily Nagoski explains that consent is expressed and revoked verbally.[21] I would add to this that sexual partners can consent only if they are conscious, as well as mentally and emotionally mature enough to understand what they are consenting to, and fully understand of any and all possible consequences of their actions. Young boys and girls who are sexually abused, then inadvertently discover that they enjoy the feeling of orgasms, are not intellectually mature enough to understand the consequences of engaging in sexual acts. This is why age of consent laws are in place.

Breaking the Silence

As a former police officer who investigated sex crimes committed against children, I'm ashamed to admit that I was previously among the population who was simply unaware that boys and men are often victims too. After I learned about the prevalence of male abuse from Mr. Kennedy, I felt compelled to research it and expose the truth—namely, that it is a hidden epidemic, and that the recognition and acknowledgement of males as victims is still in its infancy.

In recent years, significant efforts by a few people have generated some awareness of male abuse. In 1990, psychotherapist Mike Lew published the first book of its kind, *Victims No Longer: The Classic Guide for Men Recovering from Sexual Child Abuse*. Seven years later, in 1997, Sheldon Kennedy was among the first men to publicly pursue charges against his abuser. He became an educator and spoke openly to the public and professionals about his abuse experience. Three years later, his teammate Theoren Fleury followed suit. In 2002, newspapers and daytime talk shows documented the abuse of young boys by Catholic priests, resulting in a public outcry for accountability.

In 2010, Oprah Winfrey profiled 200 male survivors. Soon after professional athlete, actor, and producer Tyler Perry identified himself as a victim. Two years later the issue was highlighted again with the conviction of Jerry Sandusky, the high-profile football coach from Pennsylvania State University who had also founded a nonprofit organization for underprivileged and at-risk youth. In 2018, charges were pursued against Ohio State University after former wrestlers alleged the university ignored numerous complaints that their team doctor was a "locker-room voyeur who groped athletes" during examinations they were forced to endure.[22] Yet despite these efforts, the number of cases aired in public and the discussion around male sexual abuse remains limited.

Prevalence and Facts About Male Sexual Abuse

- A 1996 study conducted among university males (who were allowed to remain anonymous) revealed that one out of every six (approximately 18 percent) had been sexually violated before the age of 16.[23]

- In a 2005 review of studies on male victims, the US Centers for Disease Control found 16 percent had "contact childhood sexual abuse," meaning they were touched in a sexual manner.[24]

- A 2011 review of research conducted in North America and Europe also found a high prevalence of male abuse.[25]

- More recently in 2014, US researchers examined how often males acknowledged sexual victimization.[26] They defined victimization as forced or coerced sexual experiences and sexual experiences with a partner five or more years older that occurred before the age of 14. This included adult rape (defined as oral or anal intercourse obtained through threats, intoxication or violence) that occurred when the victim was 14 years or older. One of their goals was to examine males' acknowledgment of sexual assault as it correlated to being revictimized in adulthood. They placed an advertisement on Craigslist and obtained an initial sample of 323 men who agreed to fill out an online questionnaire. Of those, 120 men (37 percent) admitted to experiences that were indicative of childhood sexual assault, adult rape or both. Among those, 99 men reported experiences consistent with childhood sexual abuse, yet half of these participants did not identify themselves as having been sexually abused. Forty-five men reported behaviors consistent with adult rape, yet three-quarters of them (76 percent) did not identify the experience as a rape. Of the 99 men who reported childhood sexual abuse, 24 identified themselves as also having been raped as an adult. From this group of 24 who experienced both youth and adult abuse, only about one-third acknowledged both victimizations, and three men (13 percent) did not acknowledge either.

These findings highlight four significant points:

- The majority of males who experience abuse, either as a child or as an adult, don't recognize they've been abused.

- There are differences in reporting based on the age at which the abuse occurred. While approximately half of the males who described experiencing childhood sexual abuse acknowledged it as such, only a quarter of those who were raped as adults acknowledged it as abuse.

- Men are significantly less likely to acknowledge adult rape when it is perpetrated by a female versus a male.

- Men who said their offenders used force were more likely to label their experience as abuse.

- Despite these statistics indicating the prevalence of male sexual abuse, a 2014 review in Canada indicated that fewer than five out of every 1,000 men ever actually *reported* being sexually assaulted.[27]

Male victims who do report abuse typically wait disproportionately longer than women before disclosing.[28] Underreporting and delayed reporting have left people with the impression that male sexual abuse is rare. This is not the case. When estimating the extent of male sexual abuse, it is important to understand that official statistics likely do not capture the full scope of the problem.

Although no current US statistics on reporting could be found, past research examining what male offenders had to say about the prevalence of male abuse is quite revealing:

What Male Offenders Say About Their Crimes

- Research from 1987 focused on non-incarcerated perpetrators of male abuse who were not receiving court-ordered evaluations or treatment.[29] Participants were recruited through media advertisements, informal discussions, and formal presentations made by healthcare professionals, parole or probation officers, and forensic workers. They came from a broad socioeconomic spectrum. Many were young and well-educated (approximately 40 percent had finished at least one year of college). Each was informed that participation was voluntary and given immunity from prosecution based solely on their cooperation in the study. Participants were instructed to provide only general details of their offenses, including their preferred age and gender of victim, along with the frequency of their offenses. In total, researchers interviewed 561 perpetrators ranging in age from 13 to 76. Of these, 153 participants admitted to targeting boys outside their family. They stated that on average, they had sexually abused approximately 150 victims each. The researchers noted, "These individuals admitted to having committed the greatest number of child molestation acts against the greatest number of child victims."[30] The high percentage of child molestations committed by those who target young boys outside the home indicates the serial nature of male abuse.

Research also indicates that when compared to those who offend against female victims, the perpetrators of sexual abuse of young boys are more likely to use physical force, threats, and violence during their assaults.[31] Those who perpetrate against male victims also generally engage in their abuse more frequently and over longer periods of time.[32] Male victims also are more likely than females to have had more than one assailant.[33]

PART I

UNDERSTANDING OFFENDERS

To better appreciate the prevalence of male sexual abuse it may be helpful to understand child sexual offenders. Despite public awareness that strangers aren't the only people parents need to worry about in regard to protecting their children, many people still struggle to recognize potential offenders who don't fit the stereotypical image of a sexual predator—that being the creepy guy who sits in his van near the schoolyard offering little children candy or puppies to play with.

Parents often warn their children about not talking to strangers and about never getting into vehicles with them. While this is good advice, the problem of sexual abuse far more commonly exists much closer to home. A large majority of abused children are abused by someone they know—a relative, caregiver, or other adult who has won their trust. Given that this may be hard to comprehend, here are a few statistics that support this assertion.

In 2013, the Canadian Department of Justice conducted surveys at two centers offering support to male survivors of sexual abuse.[34] Of those who reported childhood sexual abuse, almost all of the males (57 out of 59) reported having been sexually abused as a child. Most reported that their perpetrator was someone they trusted or a family member. Thirteen were sexually abused by a family member other than a biological parent, 16 were abused by a person in authority such as a teacher, principal, babysitter or clergy and 12 were abused by a family friend. Eight were abused by their own father and three by their mother. Only four men reported having been sexually abused by a stranger.

Similarly, many of the men I spoke to were also sexually abused by a family member. Approximately half were violated by a biological parent, while a few were abused by male or female cousins or uncles. The remainder were abused by someone considered to be a family friend or someone known to their parent. Some were abused a second time by someone introduced to them by the original perpetrator. None of the men had their first experience of abuse with a stranger.

The reality is that most child sexual offenders are known (if not well known) to their victim's parent(s) or caretaker(s). I know this is difficult to comprehend; people don't generally suspect (nor want to suspect) their friends, relatives or care providers. Perpetrators know this—and count on it.

Situational or Opportunistic Child Molesters

Child sex offenders may be categorized as either situational/opportunistic or preferential, though some possess characteristics of both types. As the name implies, the situational offender are indiscriminate in that they target children (of any gender), if an opportunity presents itself. The vast majority are male (more than 97 percent), and the frequency of their offenses depends in part on their access to the victims.[35]

Preferential Child Molesters

Preferential child molesters *create* their opportunities. They are recognized as having long-term, persistent patterns of behavior that include grooming techniques which are often very well developed.[36] Preferential child molesters are much more common than situational offenders. In 1987, American psychiatrist Gene Abel conducted research on 561 offenders who admitted to an average of 150 male victims each. Among those diagnosed as pedophiles, as many as one-third (30 percent) admitted that by the time they were 13 they had already committed sexual offenses against children.[37] Having said this, it is important to distinguish that not all youths who sexually offend go on to become adult offenders. One study revealed that seven years after their initial contact with authorities, only 9 percent of youth offenders came to the attention of law enforcement agencies for sexual offenses, and only 5 percent were convicted.[38]

The preferential child molester often uses pornographic images of children to feed their sexual fantasies, much in the same way other adults use adult pornography. Some collect child pornography, then masturbate and fantasize about the material without acting out. However, in many cases arousal and fantasy fuel sexual deviance that leads to the acting out with children.[39]

Pedophiles

The term *pedophile* (also spelled *paedophile)* is reserved for those with a clinical diagnosis. According to the American Psychiatric Association's *Diagnostic and Statistical Manual of Mental Disorders* (5th ed.),[40] a person is considered a pedophile if they have recurrent fantasies about engaging in sexual activity with children, *and* they have acted on these fantasies *or* the fantasies have caused considerable disruption or personal difficulty. In other words, a person would be considered a pedophile if they spent most of their alone time viewing child pornographic images, or if they used most of their paycheck to buy child pornographic images, or if they lost their job after being caught viewing child pornographic images at work.

Around the time they enter puberty, pedophiles generally become aware of their sexual interest in children.[41] A pedophile becomes a sexual offender only when they act out sexually with children. Not all pedophiles become child molesters. The distinction is relevant since some pedophiles choose to live in celibate lifestyles and never to act on their desires.[42]

Grooming Techniques

Grooming techniques are deliberate acts and gestures which offenders, especially preferential child molesters, often engage in. The deeds, gestures and activities which are perfectly legal and not harmful in themselves, are later recognized as their offender's preparation process. They are specifically designed to win the affection, trust and loyalty of their potential victim and often the victim's parents. They are devised with the intention of helping them seduce and prepare their potential victims for future sexual relations.[43]

The grooming process begins when the predator chooses their target or goes in search of one. They will visit the places children are likely to go, including schools, arcades, shopping malls, soccer fields and parks. Sexual offenders typically study cultural trends, such as popular video games and television shows to learn about their victim's interests.[44]

Perpetrators may be very attentive to both the child's and the parents' needs in order to gain their trust, affection and loyalty.[45] Kenneth Lanning, a former FBI agent with expertise in the area of child molesters, says, "Offenders who prefer younger child victims are more likely to first 'seduce' the victim's parents/guardians to gain their trust and obtain increased access to the potential victim."[46] Their actions are carefully orchestrated with the intent to fool, manipulate and exploit the immaturity of the victim[47] as well as those meant to protect them.[48]

"The exact nature of this seduction depends in part on the developmental stages, needs, and vulnerabilities of the targeted child," Lanning says. "The skilled offender will adjust his method of deception to fit the targeted child and/or the needs of the parent."[49]

They often befriend the parents and are deceivingly transparent about their intentions to befriend their children, hoping to mislead the parent into feeling at ease with them. If they are successful, the parent(s) may begin to think, "This guy's okay. He just loves children."

Many offenders go to extreme measures, including establishing a career or hobby within an educational institution or volunteer organization. Others befriend or even marry a single parent in order to gain easy access to unguarded children. In these environments abuse often goes undetected for several years.[50]

Offenders are thought to have a radar for children in disadvantaged situations.[51] Vulnerable children include those who haven't yet learned there are people who can't be trusted, those with low self-esteem, or those in need of relationships. Rebellious teens, children and teens isolated by their peers, or those having problems with their parent(s) are easy targets. Offenders may try to win their target's affection by using self-disclosure and empathy. For example, they may tell them they too went through the same things when they were young.[52] Offenders pay special attention to those they intend to abuse. They often fake having a common background or take an interest in what interests their potential victim. They will often allow them special privileges and treat them as if they are much older than their actual age.

Sexual predators recruit victims using a variety of methods. Many are charming and offer something the child needs. They prey on weakness and vulnerability in much the same way as predators in the wild.[53] They watch for the weak individual, separate them from the group, then attack. Offenders often work to separate a child by taking the target child away from their home on educational or recreational outings.[54] They lavish the child with attention and friendship, play games with them, help them with their homework, and even assist their parents by providing rides.

Although offenders do often target disadvantaged children, the reality is any child may be abused.[55] Predators target children in healthy/average families too. Once targets are established, sexual offenders will often shower their victims with gifts, opportunities, praise and affection.[56] They work hard to find and fill any voids, often moving mountains to gain access to their victims. Any child who feels lonely, unloved or unpopular will naturally gravitate toward someone who gives them attention, affection and praise.[57]

In 2018, Lydia Lerma, a Colorado mother of three, described how convicted sex offender Andrew Vanderwal groomed her ex-husband and their young son.[58] Vanderwal, her ex-husband's roommate, helped out by picking up their six-year-old son and 12-year-old daughter from school and taking care of them while their father was at work. He also befriended other neighborhood boys who knew him as "Uncle Drew."

Vanderwal even bought their son a bike and some Nike sneakers. After his arrest, Lerma searched Vanderwal's closet. Inside she found a box and storage tubs she described as his "trophy chest." They contained a boy's baseball glove, Nerf gun, shoes, pictures of other children, photos of Andrew with other children and notes and pictures from different children. Pedophiles will often keep reminders of children they have or intend to groom, using the items as reminders or fantasy material when masturbating.

Although Lerma had the "creeps" about Vanderwal, her ex-husband didn't. Vanderwal had told him he was a pediatric medic in the Air Force and that he'd served in Afghanistan and seen horrible things, including children whom he couldn't save. His story seemed plausible. Lerma's ex-husband later said, "I looked at him like a son. Looking back, he was grooming me, too."

In the case of disadvantaged youth, the perpetrator often provides for the child's basic needs, including food, clothing, shelter and attention.[59] Retired assistant football coach Jerry Sandusky of Pennsylvania State University created his own position of trust and was well liked by members of his community. He founded a not-for-profit agency called The Second Mile, where he provided support and services for underprivileged and at-risk youth and their parents. He also adopted six children. In 2011, Sandusky was charged with 52 counts of child molestation. He was later convicted of 45 counts. He accessed his victims through his organization and coaching. A few years later one of Sandusky's adopted sons, Matthew, announced that he too, had been victimized after his adoption at eight years old and that the abuse had lasted well into his teenage years.[60]

Grooming techniques generally progress through several stages. After establishing trust predators work to increase children's acceptance of physical contact.[61] Offenders may tickle younger children, initially in front of their parents so it is deemed acceptable. In older males nonsexual touch is often encouraged first between the potential victim and one of his trusted friends. Offenders will encourage the two friends to engage in play fighting, rough play or touch sports. Once they are fully engaged the offender may or may not join in. They may encourage older boys to remove their shirts, engage in wrestling with them, or teach them how to subdue others. The first physical contact between predator and victim is often nonsexual. It is designed to desensitize the victim and get them accustomed to being touched.[62]

With boys offenders also often introduce other "masculine principles," such as the use of coarse language, which is then rewarded when used. Once they comply predators will then introduce the expectation of secrecy into their process. They may allow older children and teens to play prohibited video games or to use alcohol, tobacco or other illicit drugs while making them promise not to tell their parents.[63] They may indicate that they will both get in trouble if the boy tells. (They logically reason that it is better to be found out for offering a child alcohol or tobacco than for engaging in sexual acts.) The element of secrecy binds the victim to his predator. The expectation of secrecy may be accompanied by threats if the offender fears he may be exposed.[64] These acts help the offender to establish the risk of being reported on.

Progressively, offenders often work toward a situation in which the child has to change his clothes, spend the night or both.[65] Here the boys may be allowed to engage in other mature activities, like driving or making other adult decisions. Offenders may begin the sexual process by inquiring about their present knowledge of sex or introducing them to pornography. They will either leave magazines around for easy detection or simply give it to them.[66] The pornography may depict similar-aged children engaged in sexual acts. The gesture is designed to establish interest and provoke arousal,[67] while lessening their resistance toward engaging in such acts. Some offenders supply alcohol or drugs to lessen the inhibitions of their potential victims.[68]

Using Peer Pressure

"A child who is reluctant to engage in sexual activity with an adult or pose for sexually explicit photos can sometimes be convinced by viewing other children having fun participating in the activity. Peer pressure can have a tremendous effect on children. If other children are involved the child might be led to believe that the activity is acceptable. When pornography is used to lower inhibitions, the child portrayed will usually appear to be having a good time."[69]

Within a period of time the nonsexual touch progresses into overt sexual contact, which is the predator's ultimate goal.[70] The offender may start by offering to teach his victim about masturbation. He'll begin by telling his victim that all men masturbate, tease them about not knowing this, and then tell them they are old enough to be doing this. The offender may offer to assist them or perform oral sex on him. The increasingly inappropriate behaviors are so crafty and deceptive that the abuse is well under way before the victim recognizes he is being abused, if he ever does.

The process is progressive, sophisticated and predatory. It is employed by perpetrators and often executed so smoothly that it confuses the victims, who are reluctant to identify this "relationship" as abuse. Ultimately, perpetrators may seek to leave their victims with the belief that they liked, and even invited, the assault.[71]

The allegations depicted in the 2019 documentary *Leaving Neverland* about the late pop star Michael Jackson (who was never convicted of child abuse) show this exact scenario. Jackson is reported to have first won the trust of the parents and families of two young boys prior to isolating and abusing both of them. Jackson is portrayed as having used his status and wealth, plus his deep-seated loneliness, to woo and win the affection of both of these young boys and their families. Both boys described being in a "relationship" with Jackson and not initially recognizing that they had been groomed and sexually abused.

HOW TO RECOGNIZE A CHILD BEING GROOMED

If you see the following progressive activities occurring with an older child or an adult, especially one without children of their own, please pay attention:

- Begins to offer a child opportunities or things that seem too good to be true.
- Plans activities that eventually exclude the parent or other children.
- Requests to spend excessive amounts of time alone with a child.
- Buys a child expensive gifts or offers to take them on lavish trips.
- Encourages a child to wrestle or play fight when they are alone together.
- Asks a child to take their clothes off during sports.
- Touches them excessively during coaching.
- Invites them for sleepovers.

Make sure you have discussed the idea of grooming and abuse with your child prior to allowing them to be with older children or adults. Healthy people have healthy boundaries, especially with children.

PART 2

"THIS IS WHAT HAPPENED TO ME"

Up to this point my goal has been to provide you with a basic understanding of why males are sometimes reluctant to see themselves as victims of sexual offenders and their grooming techniques.

What follows are the personal stories of each of the men I interviewed. I discuss how their abuse began, their relationship to their abusers, and how the abuse was maintained. Also included are their specific explanations of why they did not disclose their abuse sooner. My hope is that as you learn about these men's experiences, you become more aware of the fact that male sexual abuse happens far more commonly than most people understand—and that it is far more damaging than was previously understood. Their deeply personal stories are intended to provide both context and insights into how, where and when male sexual abuse occurs. As you read their stories you will begin to see the barriers to seeking help faced by these boys and men. You will hear why many boys and men who have been abused don't discuss it with anyone, and learn how facing their trauma alone impacted them as children and as adults. You will also come to see that the long-term damage caused by sexual abuse can be profound.

The names used are pseudonyms and any personal information that would reveal an individual's identity or the identity of their abuser has been changed or withheld. However, the details of their abuse stories have not been altered or embellished. All of the stories are relayed as they were told to me.

The Men

Aaron: "I Didn't Know Much About Sex"

Aaron was 55 at the time of his interview. Prior to his abuse, he had never spoken to his family or friends about sexual matters. By junior high he still didn't know much about sex, and had very little interest in it compared to his peers. By most standards, he was a late bloomer. "When I started high school I was the youngest kid in the class. I hadn't developed yet. I hit puberty really late. I was 15."

When Aaron was 14 he attended a week-long basketball camp about 60 miles from his home. His older brother had previously attended the same camp, and the coach who was the camp director was also a friend of the family. Aaron looked up to him. "He was a tough guy, he made us work really hard and be responsible for what we did. He sent us all these really good messages." Aaron enjoyed being around him. When camp was over his coach commended him for being the hardest working kid in camp and invited him to stay behind after everyone else left to help take the camp down. This meant Aaron would be alone with him for the next several days until the job was done. Aaron asked his parents if he could stay and admits he was excited but nervous when they agreed.

After everyone left Aaron's coach began to treat him differently—less like a kid and more like an adult. He taught Aaron how to drive and let him drive a vehicle alone, even though he didn't have a license. He gave him alcohol and then asked him what he knew about sex. No adult had ever talked to him about sex before.

His coach then introduced him to pornography. "He was telling me this is what it means to be a man, that he knows a lot about me, like that I'm already [masturbating] a few times a week. He basically said, 'Take those magazines and go in the bathroom and do what you're supposed to do.'"

Although the conversation made him very nervous, Aaron enjoyed being treated like a man, and he complied. He didn't know that the coach had peepholes in the bathroom, shower, and where he slept at night. The next night the coach gave Aaron more magazines to take to his room. He watched Aaron through the peepholes, so he knew precisely when to walk in and catch him masturbating. The coach reassured him that what he was doing was natural, and then left him alone again with more magazines, which were more graphic and contained images of men engaging in sexual acts with other men.

The next time the coach walked in he told Aaron he was going to show him what guys really do when they're alone, and he proceeded to fondle, masturbate, and engage in oral sex with Aaron.

Aaron was shocked. "I didn't know what molestation was. I didn't know it could happen to boys."

When Aaron attempted to protest by asking his coach if he was trying to "make him gay," the coach got violently mad and told him not to talk like that. Aaron's abuse continued for the next several days until the coach finally drove him home. The coach then insisted Aaron shake his hand, and said goodbye as if nothing happened. He even went inside and spoke to both of Aaron's parents and shook their hands.

HOW OFFENDERS PREPARE THEMSELVES

Aside from grooming both the victim and the parent, offenders may also need to rationalize (to themselves) the crimes they are about to commit. They may try to convince themselves that the sexual acts they are about to commit are pleasurable or at least not harmful to the child. They may tell themselves that the child needs to understand sexual matters, or if they are young enough, that they won't remember the acts.[72]

After, they may rationalize their behavior as an expression of their love, or tell themselves they are entitled to use them because of all the good they do for them.

Aaron didn't say anything.

"There was a bathroom on the first floor. It didn't have any windows. I got in there, closed the door, turned the lights off, turned the shower on and just … cried." Aaron tried to "wash off" his abuse, but he couldn't.

Although Aaron had wanted to tell his parents, he was too ashamed, too afraid, too upset, and too confused. He especially wanted to tell his father but felt he couldn't. He knew his parents thought very highly of the coach. He also knew that he had participated in several activities he knew his parents wouldn't approve of.

"I was a perfect victim because my parents didn't talk to me about sex," Aaron said." I wanted to tell my father, but I knew that if I told him he'd tell my mother, and I'd get in trouble."

Aaron also was confused. He felt as if his body had betrayed him. He hadn't had any previous sexual interest in males, but since he'd experienced erections and orgasm several times, he questioned whether he'd participated willingly.

After returning home Aaron distanced himself from his mother. Although they had previously been very close and he loved his mother, he feared he might accidentally tell her what happened or that she would somehow figure it out. He knew that if she found out she'd be devastated. He didn't want to hurt her so he remained silent.

"My mother kept saying, 'What's wrong?' and 'You were always such a happy kid. What happened? Why are you so sad?'" Aaron recalled. "I just pushed her away. I was afraid of her finding out."

When Aaron went back to school he went to see his guidance counselor, a priest.

"I was trying to talk to him about it, but I wasn't saying it, just, you know, you have to warn the kids that go to that camp about the director," Aaron said. "And he was like, 'Why? What are you talking about?' I was like, 'You just got to warn them about him.'"

Aaron didn't actually tell the priest what happened, but he believes the priest understood what he was implying. The counselor's response was to 'absolve' Aaron of his sins and tell him never to discuss it with anyone again. Looking back, Aaron believes, "He knew exactly what I meant and he wanted me to shut up about it. He's the one that sent me to the camp in the first place." Aaron's guidance counselor was later determined to also be abusing young boys.

As a young man, Aaron didn't understand or recognize this. Instead, he was left with the sense it was somehow his fault. Confused and upset, Aaron didn't talk about his abuse again for several years. He became negative, isolated himself, and avoided serious or emotional conversations. He dressed in oversized clothes and tried to hide. Fortunately, Aaron found track and field and was very good at it. He became the MVP of his school's track team, which he said helped balance out his feelings of confusion.

In his later years of high school, his relationships remained shallow. He preferred to talk to girls on the phone rather than take them out on dates because he worried they would somehow "know" and out him for being "damaged goods."

Years later, when Aaron was in college, his abuser contacted his mother to "check up" on Aaron. She innocently gave him Aaron's new number, telling her son, "That nice man, that director from camp wanted your number, so I gave it to him. What a nice guy to be following up with you all these years later."

Aaron cringed. "I just felt so disgusted, horrible, invaded. I thought I had gotten away from it, and then it became like I'm never going to escape this. I felt terrible. My mother innocently thought, oh, here's this man of God trying to reach out to me and be a good person. It was just so disgusting."

Aaron's mother passed away a short while later. She never learned the truth about why Aaron had chosen to distance himself from her.

By the time Aaron graduated from law school he had already assisted in the prosecution of one male child sexual abuse case. He had not yet filed his documents to become a full member of the state bar association when his older brother contacted him.

"He said, 'Listen, I just saw this movie, *Something About Amelia.*' Now that you're a prosecutor, we need to do something about the director of the camp.'"

Aaron was shocked. He had no idea that his brother knew about his coach and the abuse. But he actually didn't know. As Aaron listened his brother explained that once when he was at the same camp, when no one was around, he snuck into the coach's office. Inside he found three large paper bags filled with polaroid pictures of the coach molesting boys.

Aaron responded, "Holy f***! I thought I was the only one!" His brother was now the one to be shocked. He hadn't known Aaron was among those who had been victimized, only that many others had been abused by the coach.

Aaron asked why he hadn't told him or the police about the pictures sooner. His brother explained that the coach had caught him in his office and threatened him with a gun. He pointed it at him, pulled the trigger and said, "It would be that easy." Aaron's brother believed the threat to be real and remained silent.

The day after his brother phoned him Aaron went to the FBI. Although he was shaking and embarrassed, he told his story. The FBI asked if he would be willing to wear a recording device and try to talk to the coach, but Aaron refused.

"I said, 'No f***ing way.' I'd have nightmares about running into him. I said, 'There's no way I'm sitting down and having a civil conversation with this guy. I mean, he's evil.'"

The agents told Aaron that without his help the investigation might not go anywhere. Nonetheless, they continued to investigate. The FBI learned the coach had taught at 13 different Catholic schools in 23 years, and that there was an allegation of abuse at each one. Every time an allegation came up he resigned and went to a new school. They interviewed all the teams he coached, but due to the statute of limitations they were unable to identify any offenses that had occurred recently enough to lay charges. They needed information about any possible new offenses— information that Aaron may be in a position to obtain.

Even though he was already working with a prosecution unit, Aaron had put off filing his bar association paperwork because the process required him to list every place he'd ever lived, and he didn't want to admit he had spent the summer at the basketball camp. He was worried that if someone else from the camp came forward — he might somehow be identified as a victim.

When Aaron's boss threatened to fire him if he didn't get his registration completed, Aaron finally began the process. One of the requirements was that he provide university transcripts to show that he had actually successfully completed his law degree. He filled out a request to obtain the documents and submitted it to the school registrar's office. Later, when he went to pick up his transcripts, he was shocked to see his coach sitting behind the desk working as the night clerk. He had accepted a job working security at the same university Aaron had attended.

"I felt like I was in the twilight zone. I'd just convinced myself that he would never know about me, that I was being a ridiculous, foolish child, that I don't ever have to worry about him again, and there he is sitting there. The first thing out of his mouth was, 'Yeah, I noticed you graduated from here a couple years ago.' It was my worst nightmare. He had just gotten the job two weeks earlier. It was a total coincidence. So, I went into the dean's office, gave her my application, and told her to handle it personally."

When Aaron walked back out, the coach commented, "Oh by the way, sorry to hear about your mother's death." This enraged Aaron so much that he went outside, picked up the phone, called the FBI and said, "I know where he is right now. Come and wire me up."

The FBI was happy to do this. They needed evidence of more recent offenses and instructed Aaron about what to say. They suggested he tell the coach that he needed to talk to him about something "very private" and to pretend that he too had an interest in young boys. Although the thought repulsed Aaron, he cooperated.

"We met at a bar at 10:30 at night." The coach asked Aaron what he wanted to talk about. "I'm like, 'Give me a minute, let me drink a bit, you know, I'm really nervous about this. I've never talked to anybody about it before.'" Aaron's coach began to reset the power difference by berating him: "Well, you always were a wimp. You never could stand on your own two feet."

Aaron understood what the coach was trying to do. "I realized what was going on and I played into it. I was like, 'Well, I just don't know if I can tell you, I'm not sure.'" Aaron's coach took the bait. "He goes, 'This has to do with sex, right?'" Aaron said it did. His coach added, "And it has to do with kids." Aaron played along, "Oh my God, how do you know?" Aaron's coach fell into the role completely, responding, "Well, let me just tell you this, I'm the teacher here. You listen, but correct me if I'm wrong."

Aaron's offender proceeded to tell him about how he first began offending against boys. He said he got started when he was a teen volunteer at a children's shelter. He said it was easy, that he simply accessed the boys at night when nobody else was around.

The FBI had told Aaron what might happen if Aaron did as they asked and faked an interest in offending against young boys. His offender would most likely brag about how he got away with it so many times and say that he'd be proud to teach Aaron how to do the same. Halfway through their first conversation Aaron's offender said, "I got to tell you … of all my boys, you're the last one I ever expected to come back to me."

When Aaron asked him why, the coach replied, "Because I was hard on you, I hit you hard. I came back again and again, and I knew by your reaction that you weren't taking it well, so I should have been kinder or something like that."

Aaron responded about having been "just a kid" who didn't really understand "that kind of stuff." His offender bought it and kept talking.

Unfortunately, he only spoke about offenses that were way outside of the statute of limitations. Aaron had to meet with him six times before he finally got any information about a more recent offense.

"He showed me a picture of the kid with a basketball uniform which had his number and stuff. I told the agent, and they investigated it. They eventually arrested him and he pled guilty. He got a five-year split sentence, which means he spent less than 18 months in jail. He sent all his family members postcards saying he was on sabbatical, you know, to cover up the fact that he was in jail for molesting boys. He had something like 100 victims. In one school where he taught there were 13 boys in the class and he molested 11 of them. It was just horrible."

During the investigation Aaron found out that even though his coach had been kicked out of seminary school the Catholic Church still let him run the youth camp and teach high school. He also learned that the guidance counselor he'd gone to after his abuse was also abusing kids in his school at the same time.

In the end, despite his fears, Aaron played a crucial role in catching and convicting his own offender. When the investigation was over the FBI offered Aaron a job as a police officer. He accepted, and in the years that followed worked his way into the same unit that handled his offender's case.

These days Aaron has a successful career that has nothing to do with law. He identifies as bisexual, but wonders if he would have been heterosexual if he had not been abused.

"I questioned, 'why did he pick me out of all the kids in the world, all the boys'? Something must be wrong with me. He must know something about me that I don't know. I had guys who were really close friends. I didn't have sexual thoughts about them, but after being molested, it began invading my fantasy life. Like when I was 15, and I'm in the locker room and, wait a minute, why am I looking at that kid?"

As Aaron got older his confusion continued.

"I had a number of sexual relationships with women, and every one of them ended in her cheating on me. So, I thought, I know the reason! She knows fundamentally what's wrong with me. She cheated on me because I just don't measure up. I felt horrible as a man. I felt horrible as a lover. It was terrible. Eventually I would come to the conclusion that I had to find out if this is true about me or not: Am I gay?"

RE-WRITING THEIR OWN STORIES

Child victims, even after becoming adults, often either deny their victimization or disclose it in inaccurate but more socially acceptable ways. They do so because they suffer from varying degrees of shame, guilt, and embarrassment. Society tells them in so many ways they are not "real victims.[81]"

"I didn't do anything sexually for at least six years. I thought that was a vampire bite. I thought it was a fait accompli," Aaron said. "I thought that's how it happened, that's how people got gay."

Aaron decided to test himself and date men. He worried that if he didn't learn to accept being gay, he would commit suicide.

Later, at the coach's sentencing, Aaron confronted him. To his amazement, the coach again tried to shake Aaron's hand, and said, "You didn't have to do this, I was going to quit teaching.'" Aaron responded, "Bullshit. You still think I am a stupid kid. I am gonna be watching you for the rest of your miserable life."

Aaron's coach never got another job working with kids. This encounter was the start of Aaron viewing his abuser as a very "pathetic, sick, criminal man" rather than an evil monster that held any power over him. "That was really important."

THE IMPACT OF MALE CHILD SEXUAL ABUSE ON GENDER IDENTITY AND SEXUAL ORIENTATION

Richard Gartner, a psychologist known for his work with male victims of sexual trauma, believes that when male child sexual abuse is perpetrated by another male, it can undermine the victim's sense of gender identity and sexual orientation.[73]

Whether the victim is straight or not, childhood sexual abuse perpetrated by other males leaves victims confused about their masculine identity and about whether or not they have homosexual tendencies.[74] Male survivors often confuse doubt about their masculinity and potential homosexuality with the shame they feel about having been victimized. Many truly believe they somehow invited the abuse by expressing homosexual inclinations.

Gay men ask whether they invited the abuse and liked it, or if the abuse made them gay. They often confuse sexual abuse with an initiation into adulthood, a coming-of-age experience or an affair.[75] Similarly, heterosexual boys abused by male perpetrators often view their arousal as a sign that deep down they are actually gay or will become gay.[76] Many straight males overcompensate through hyper-masculinity and homophobia; others choose to live in isolation.[77]

Childhood sexual abuse perpetrated by females is also confused with a coming-of-age experience.[78] One researcher posits that young men who would have been headed toward heterosexual relationships are so repulsed by their early sexual activities at the hands of a person they were not attracted to that they reject their natural heterosexual orientation and redefine themselves as gay or become asexual.[79]

Since men have a preoccupation with sex and are socialized to believe they should never turn it down, many are forced to think of the abuse as something they should have enjoyed.[80]

Ricky: "I Liked the Attention"

Ricky (49) was born hearing impaired. His mother had significant health issues of her own, so Ricky's hearing loss went undetected until he was evaluated prior to entering kindergarten. After several surgeries, Ricky gained the ability to hear for the first time in his life. He was five years old. Excited about his new "superpower," he decided to take up drumming.

He began taking lessons from Denny, a 19-year-old who lived down the street. Denny had a sister who was cognitively impaired. Denny had previously bribed her with candy to kiss Ricky. Ricky thought very little of it until after his second or third drum lesson. Although he cannot recall what happened at the lessons, he remembers coming home, destroying his drum set and telling his parents he didn't want any more drum lessons. He never went back.

Soon after, he began wetting his bed and having nightmares about being trapped in Denny's house. Shortly thereafter, Denny's older brother was killed in the Vietnam War. Ricky remembers wishing it was himself who had died instead.

Around the same time, Ricky's mother, who had multiple sclerosis and several other significant health issues, became wheelchair dependent, so his parents made the decision to move to a more wheelchair-accessible house in the suburbs. Because his mother was not capable of caring for him, Ricky stayed behind in the house to live with his grandmother. She had a gambling addiction and paid very little attention to Ricky, who visited his parents only on weekends and holidays and for short periods during the summer.

This arrangement worked until Ricky's mother took a turn for the worse, and even his summer visits became too much for his parents to handle. Subsequently, when Ricky was 11, his father sent him overseas to Italy to stay with an aunt and cousin who both spoke Italian. Although Ricky spoke some Italian he wasn't fluent, so he felt like the odd person out.

While in Italy, Ricky's cousin, who was five years his senior, offered to take Ricky camping with a group of his friends. This is when Ricky had his second sexual abuse experience. On the first night of a six-day camping trip, Ricky had fallen asleep in the tent while lying next to his cousin. He woke up when he felt his cousin begin to fondle him. Ricky was confused.

"I didn't know what to do. I mean, it wasn't as if I couldn't physically push him away. But I was scared and I froze, so he continued to fondle me." Ricky hoped it would stop if he didn't respond, but it didn't. The fondling continued until Ricky ejaculated. This confused him more. "I mean it felt good. It's a physical release. But at the same time, it scared me and grossed me out. I felt weird, really scared and disgusted."

Confused by what had happened, Ricky chose not to say anything about the abuse when they awoke the next morning. They both simply went about their business as if nothing had happened.

Ricky secretly hoped it would never happen again, but it did the next night. This time his cousin assaulted him more aggressively, pushing Ricky to engage in oral sex. Ricky objected but his cousin was bigger, stronger and more determined, and he succeeded in getting what he wanted. Ricky felt powerless to stop it. He was in a foreign country where he didn't speak the language and had little control over his own environment.

PARADOXICAL BEHAVIORS

Victims are often confused by the contradictory acts of being cared for and being violated by the same person.[82] Inevitably, one consequence of child sexual abuse is a betrayal of trust. This betrayal along with the sexual abuse can leave victims feeling guilt and confusion over having "wanted" the relationship or their level of "cooperation." All children have wants, needs, and desires. What they really want and need are healthy, nonsexual relationships.[83] Sexual abuse is always damaging.

Ricky's cousin was the only member of his family who'd ever paid any real attention to him. At the time, he thought, "He's taking an interest in me, actually showing me some affection and consideration." Ricky had been lonely and enjoyed the attention. It felt nice. Reflecting back, he said, "I don't know if I'd say I 'let' it happen, but I didn't fight it as much. It felt good physically, it felt good emotionally. I didn't realize he was using me."

Ricky's cousin then invited his friends to join in, and the abuse escalated and continued until his visit to Italy came to an end. Ricky was happy to be going home until he learned that his cousin planned to move to America. The cousin moved in with an aunt who lived near Ricky, and the abuse continued for the next several years.

WAS I REALLY A VICTIM?

Many men struggle to accept that they are victims.[84] In Western society, men tend to disown their vulnerabilities, protect their image of masculinity, and disregard the impact of sexual abuse on their lives.[85] Many adopt myths about having enjoyed the abuse.[86] They sometimes choose to rewrite their original memories and regard themselves as "lucky," even convince themselves that they were, in fact, in control of the situation. They may even discuss their abuse experience with others but tell the story as if it were something they enjoyed. As they do this they are attempting to change how they *really* feel about what happened. Many go so far as to shame themselves for being so afraid. These reactions complicate how men process and heal from the traumas they experienced as children and youth. What began as abuse remains abuse; children cannot consent to sexual activities.

In Ricky's eyes, at that point, the abuse he experienced became more consensual. He was initially reluctant to even label it as abuse. He minimized the fact that he had been traumatized and disgusted and that he had tried to stop the assaults. Instead, he focused on the fact that he had enjoyed the attention he got from his cousin and the physiological sensation of ejaculation. When his cousin tried to force him into more aggressive acts, Ricky ended the abuse. "Oral sex is one thing, but anal sex—that ain't happening, not without a gun to my head."

Ricky ended the abusive relationship when he was 18 but didn't talk about it for years. He now recognizes the abuse as abuse and understands that it was extremely damaging. He also sees that it occurred during a time in his childhood when he desperately needed attention, affection and physical contact.

When asked about what influenced his decision not to inform his parents about the abuse, Ricky said he felt like his parents already had enough problems to deal with because of his mother's poor health. He also didn't think his father, whom he described as extremely religious and homophobic, would understand.

ABUSE OFTEN LEADS TO CONFUSION

Confused Non-Compliant. Amid the memories of having been afraid, many men also recall having enjoyed the physical release associated with having an orgasm, then experience shame. Since their bodies responded physically to the stimulation they question if they enjoyed being abused? The answer is still no. It's natural to enjoy having an orgasm, our bodies are wired that way.

Emotionally in Need Non-Compliant. Many groomed males recall having enjoyed the relationship (outside of the sexual aspect) and subsequently choosing not to sever the bond, despite the sexual abuse. They may recall choosing to fight less or "allowing" the abuse to continue. What started as abuse is still abuse.

Fatigued Non-Compliant. Despite their initial fear and terror, boys often submit to their perpetrator because they realize it is futile to fight; they know they will be overpowered. Others submit because they come to understand that if they cooperate the abuse will end sooner or the perpetrator will decrease their level of violence. Abuse is abuse, despite the victim's level of resistance.

Ricky feared his father would overreact, shut down or simply tell him just to get over it. Or, he might not believe him. What Ricky was going through was upsetting enough; he didn't want to have to deal with his father's reaction as well.

As a result, Ricky didn't speak to anyone about the abuse for several years. He wanted to avoid a family feud and protect what little sense of family he had. He also reasoned that if he couldn't tell his own parents, there was no one else he could tell.

Jacob: "How Could I Do That?"

Jacob (63) who was severely abused by his mother, was confused by his body's response to being abused. He apologized for what he was about to disclose and stated it may be hard to believe. He said he understood this since even he had difficulty comprehending the magnitude of what took place in his infancy and youth.

"I'm sitting here because I am a survivor and I want to help," he stated.

Jacob didn't remember when his abuse first began, only that he was very little, too young to go to school, when his mother began engaging in sexual acts, including intercourse, with him. He had also been raped by multiple other people, including his priest and a man with whom his father worked, plus those his mother had sent him to. Jacob's mother sold him and forced him to work as a child prostitute.

During the abuse, his mother often spoke about Jacob's kindness, tenderness and specialness. Her words left him confused and feeling as if he somehow was responsible for the abuse. In addition to being forced to have sex with her, Jacob's mother sent him to the homes of other women in their neighborhood. These women would pay for access to Jacob, who would go to their houses alone and then bring home the money he had "earned." Adding to his considerable distress, his mother sometimes accused Jacob of keeping portions of the money for himself and berated him for being "dishonest" and "selfish."

Jacob was abused like this for several years. He believes that his father knew but turned a blind eye to his son's trauma. Jacob speculates that his father may have enjoyed the extra money or was happy to be relieved of his sexual duties as a husband. Although Jacob's father never abused him sexually, he berated Jacob verbally and threatened him with violence. Jacob had two siblings: a younger sister, whom Jacob believes was never abused, and a twin brother, Jack, who had a mental disability. Jacob did his best to protect his brother from their mother whenever she approached him.

Unfortunately, the physical and sexual abuse perpetrated by Jacob's parents set the stage for further abuse outside the home. Jacob believes he became known as a boy who could be used for sex. Jacob's father, who worked in the engine room of a docked ship, took Jacob to work with him one day. His father left him alone briefly and a guy "came out of nowhere," pulled Jacob's pants down and threw him up against the inspection port while he anally raped him. Jacob recalled, "He was very rough, then tucked my shirt in, pulled my pants up. My father came around the corner, yelled something, then came over." Although both Jacob and his assailant acted as if nothing had happened, Jacob's father didn't believe them. He beat the man badly and told Jacob to sit where he could keep an eye on him for the rest of the day, but never offered Jacob any solace.

Jacob described his grandmother as his only source of comfort, love and compassion as a child. He loved her deeply. Even though she could be cold at times, Jacob enjoyed her company and liked to go to church with her. One day after the service, when he was six or seven, his grandmother walked in on their priest anally raping Jacob in a back room of their church.

"I was bent over and my grandmother came around the corner, and it was like I was shocked I got caught, like it was my fault." Jacob then realized, "I wasn't making a sound, I wasn't crying, I wasn't doing anything because it had happened I don't know how many times before."

HABITUATION

Habituation is a form of learning whereby a victim's emotional and physical responses to trauma will decrease if the trauma is repeated or prolonged. It is like a defeat response after becoming desensitized.[87] This doesn't mean a victim is not harmed, but rather that their trauma response system has gone off so many times in the past without rescue that it adapts to being defeated and stops responding.

Jacob's grandmother did nothing to stop the abuse, though she did have her husband check on her grandson later. "I was in the kitchen because I was allowed to eat as much as I wanted at my grandparents' house 'cause there wasn't lots of food at home," Jacob said. "I was coming back from the refrigerator, and my grandfather got up from his chair and came into the kitchen. I froze. He asked me, 'Do you want me to take a look? You okay down there? You want me to check?'"

Jacob declined and told his grandfather that he was okay. His grandfather then explained that there was nothing they could do about what had happened since the man who had raped Jacob was their priest.

It got worse. Later, when Jacob's grandparents told his parents about what had happened, his parents forbade Jacob from seeing his grandparents again. This loss devastated Jacob because it deprived him of the only place where he ever felt safe. From this experience, Jacob learned that no one would help him, and that if he tried to get help that things would just get worse. He didn't see his grandparents again for several years until he was old enough to ride his bike to their house, which was 15 miles away. The first time Jacob showed up his grandparents were shocked and told Jacob that he wasn't supposed to be there. He told them not to tell on him and continued visiting them whenever he could.

When he was about eight years old, Jacob came to see his mother as "crazy." One example of her craziness occurred when she sent Jacob and his brother outside to cut the lawn with scissors. That's when he began to count the years until he would be old enough to move out on his own. "I remember saying, 10 more years and I am outta here." He believed that if he was going to survive until adulthood it was up to him, that no one else was ever going to help him.

DISSOCIATION

People who experience repeated traumatic events or overwhelming events often freeze or dissociate.[88] Dissociation is a natural physiological response to being traumatized. It is one of the body's natural defense mechanisms, intended to minimize the impact of otherwise unbearable events.

Dissociation involves a mental, emotional, and physiological detachment or disengagement from one's own consciousness or immediate surroundings (kind of like being in a dream state). When victims perceive they cannot tolerate or escape what is happening, they dissociate. This can protect victims in the short term, but over the long term it has the potential to disrupt every area of psychological functioning.

Dissociation occurs on a spectrum. Mild forms include "zoning out" or daydreaming, a state that can also be entered into voluntarily. More intense forms include feeling as if not present in the current time, feeling "unreal," or not recognizing oneself in the mirror. Stronger, more pathological forms of dissociation include the development of "alters" (other personalities) designed to endure the trauma. This is called dissociative identity disorder (described later).

By the time he entered third grade, Jacob was dissociating very badly and thus doing very poorly in school. For doing poorly, Jacob's parents would beat him, which made it even harder for him to concentrate the following day.

"It was sh*t. I mean it was real shi*t. I can remember being scrunched up in a ball, hugging my knees and saying to myself, 'I'm not going to feel anything. They're not going to get to me. I'm not going to feel a thing. It doesn't matter what they say or do. It's not going to hurt.'"

CONSEQUENCES OF DISSOCIATION

Dissociating can greatly impact a child's ability to pay attention in school. A dissociated child will have less capacity to attend to auditory cues, and their ability to think clearly and to make decisions, act appropriately, or complete assignments is diminished. This can wreak havoc in a classroom, where making decisions, paying attention, and responding appropriately are critical to a child's learning, confidence, and progression through school. Many victims of childhood sexual abuse also have a diminished ability to pay attention due to the loss of sleep they experience. If they are abused at night or having nightmares, falling asleep can feel very unsafe.

In fourth grade, Jacob had art class once a week and was allowed to draw whatever he wanted. One day after he got home, his parents were arguing over something he had painted. All Jacob recalled was that he had drawn "black." He told his parents it was the swamp on the way to school. They beat him for having drawn attention to himself at school with the painting.

The next week, his art teacher sat him away from the other students and told him that he could draw whatever he wanted. He refused to draw, saying, "I don't want to do anything. I'm fine." When his teacher said, "I just don't understand why some parents have kids," Jacob grew afraid that she might know something wasn't right at home. He didn't say anything since interventions in the past had only made things worse.

Jacob and his family lived in a rural part of their community and Jacob often needed to hitchhike to school. Men from his community would often offer him a ride under the guise of being helpful, but with ulterior motives. Jacob experienced several attempted rapes while he was simply trying to get to and from school. He stated that he became very good at jumping out of moving vehicles, at stop signs, and red lights until electric locks were invented.

When Jacob was in seventh grade, he experienced one particularly frightening event, which he reported to his school's vice principal:

"A guy tried hauling me into his car, but I got out and made it to the bus," he said. "When I got to school, I went to the principal's office and reported it. Around 1:00, the vice principal came and called me out of class and brought me into the office."

Jacob could see through the door that his mother was in the next office talking to somebody else. "She had a wig on and bright red makeup." Jacob almost didn't recognize her. He asked when he could talk to her but was told she didn't want to talk to him. Jacob was sent back to class. "I remember sitting in Spanish class thinking, 'Geez, I guess it's no big deal.'"

Although the principal had called his mother the incident was not brought to the attention of the police, nor was it brought up again at school or at home. His principal's failure to respond confirmed Jacob's belief that he should never attempt to trust anyone again.

Jacob described earlier incidents when the principal had witnessed situations that were either neglectful or indicative of abuse and had again failed to intervene. One time his mother had passed out drunk in the car after arriving to pick up Jacob and his siblings from school. Jacob had tried to wake her but couldn't, so he ran and told his principal that he thought his mother was dead.

"He told me go stand with my brother and sister and all of a sudden, a shouting match occurred between the two of them. He told us to get in the car! She was drunk out of her mind and she drove us home. Nobody did anything. It was never brought up again."

A CHILD'S CHANGED PERCEPTION OF THE WORLD

Sexual assaults, when perpetrated by someone a child depends on or trusts, can have a significant negative impact on their ability to trust others. Childhood sexual abuse can impact how a child views themselves and the world around them. The experience of being sexually abused can transform a child's previous perception of the world from that of a safe and predictable place to a terror-filled, confusing place. Childhood sexual abuse can also seriously impact a child's ability to form healthy relations later in life. This is especially true if the perpetrator threatened to harm or kill them or their siblings as a means of ensuring their silence. The impact of trauma on a child is commonly far greater than the impact on an adult.[89]

In the end, Jacob's grandparents, principal, football coach, doctor, and a teacher each had reasons to suspect he was being neglected and abused but failed to intervene.

When asked how his abuse ended, Jacob explained that one day after he'd come home from a house across the street his father asked him why he was going to the neighbors all the time. Jacob lied and said he went to see their puppies. His father knew he was lying and forbade him from ever going there again and moved his family to the other side of town. Jacob was 14 when they moved. By the time they moved, Jacob had grown and became physically able to defend himself against his mother when she approached him. Although the sexual abuse ended, the physical abuse by his father continued for another three years until he was finally strong enough to stand up to him as well. He described the day it happened:

"My father came at me. He's a big guy and he had backed me up against a workbench in the garage, and he had his hand cocked. I said to him, 'Before you hit me, you better see where my hands are. I guarantee when I hit you, you're not getting up.'" Jacob had reached into an open drawer and had his hand on some hammers and files. His father laughed at him but backed off. "I would have killed him. I was totally okay that I'd go to jail. I just didn't give a f***."

When Jacob was 21 he married an abusive woman. She verbally abused him and mirrored many of his mother's behaviors. He described her as an alcoholic and drug addict with borderline personality disorder, whom he stayed married to for four years.

He married a second time in his thirties and had two boys. It was at this point that Jacob finally started to reach out for help. As a father, he didn't want to repeat his parents' mistakes. He sought therapy after learning his son had cancer and needed a bone marrow transplant. He did not discuss his abuse.

In his late fifties, Jacob sought therapy again. After two years, at age 59, he finally disclosed his history of abuse. Unfortunately, this therapist died shortly after his disclosure. She was the first person Jacob had ever told. Jacob began working with a new therapist and was diagnosed with post-traumatic stress disorder (PTSD).

As an adult, Jacob speculated about his father. "Now I'm seeing the bigger picture," he said. "Maybe he knew my mother was raping me and was pimping me out, and that's why he was so angry with me. She would blame me for things and tell my father. He liked whips and fists."

Jacob still firmly believes he did the right thing remaining silent. He doesn't believe the necessary social supports existed at that time. He is now fully engaged in treatment with a new therapist he trusts, and at the time of our interview he was in a healthy relationship with a kind, patient and supportive woman.

POST-TRAUMATIC STRESS DISORDER (PTSD)

PTSD is a *brain injury* that some people develop after experiencing (or witnessing) life-threatening events. PTSD consists of common symptoms of trauma that do not remit with the passing of time. Common symptoms include:

- Re-experiencing the trauma or feeling as if the traumatic event(s) were happening again in the present time (flashback).

- Being physiologically and emotionally activated, or experiencing a surge of emotions and physiological responses when reminded of the traumatic events.

- Difficulty falling or staying asleep or having re-occurring nightmares.

- Feeling more irritable or having outbursts of anger.

- Feeling constantly edgy or "on guard" as if danger is lurking around every corner.

- Avoidance of places, things or thoughts that remind them of the traumatic event(s).

- A loss of interest in taking part in previously important and/or fun social activities.

- Feeling numb or having difficulty experiencing positive feelings.

Flashbacks are intense sensory images that occur involuntarily in the victim's mind. Having a flashback is like having a nightmare when you are awake. The images are vivid and emotionally upsetting. They cause victims to mentally re-experience their traumatic events, often with the same intensity of emotion and physiological reactivity they experienced when the trauma first occurred. (This is called being activated or triggered, which is discussed later.)

People with untreated PTSD feel physiological distress and constantly search for danger. They often feel an overall lack of safety and go to significant effort to avoid people, places or things that remind them of traumatic events. They lose interest in important and positive activities and have difficulty experiencing positive feelings like happiness, joy, and love until their PTSD is treated.

Anthony: "Talk About It and It Will Kill You"

Anthony, 62, was a gentle and mild-mannered man who also had been badly physically and emotionally abused by both of his parents and sexually abused by his father. He believes it must have begun before he was two years old, since his earliest memories are of being abused.

His father's abuse included an act called "fisting," which means that he inserted his closed fist into his young son's anus. Anthony was forced to endure this act during bath time. He didn't know it was abuse, he thought it was just bathing.

Anthony's mother suffered from clinical depression and psychosis. She spent most of her time in her bedroom with the door closed.

"My mother was a drug addict. She was on prescription drugs for most of my life. I don't really know what she knew, what she understood, but she was very ill. I mean, obviously my father's very ill, but my father could pass for sane. My mother never could. My father was popular and had friends and people liked him. My mother was the odd woman he married."

Anthony described his mother as abusive as well as emotionally neglectful. He learned very early that if she was in her bedroom, he needed to avoid her or risk being beaten.

Outside of his home life, Anthony was isolated and lonely. He spent most of his youth in "a high level of distress" with little ability to relate to his peers. He described himself as extremely dysregulated, the "weird kid" that everyone else avoided.

When Anthony was seven or eight, he beat another child who had provoked him.

"It was a big thing. They came to interview me, and I was clueless. I said, 'He got hurt? Really?' I mean I knew I didn't like the kid, and I knew we had fights, but I didn't remember beating him. There was another incident. I don't know what happened that time either, but a kid jumped on my back, and I put that kid in the hospital. Then all the other kids were furious at me."

DYSREGULATION

When people are physiologically or emotionally dysregulated, they are unable to regulate (tolerate or control) their own emotions. Dysregulated children may act impulsively and be hyper-aroused one minute, then withdrawn, unemotional and flat the next.

Being dysregulated can wreak havoc on a child's ability to form relationships and succeed in life. Dysregulated children are often deemed to be poor or weak students. They are sometimes misdiagnosed with ADD or ADHD instead of being understood as victims of trauma.

Anthony developed a deep self-loathing that he didn't understand. "I was starting to come apart," he said. "When I was 10, I started to kill my pets, and that made me feel worse about myself."

REACTIVE ATTACHMENT DISORDER

In the absence of adequate caregiving or extreme emotional neglect, children may develop a disorder known as reactive attachment disorder, which is characterized by depressive symptoms and withdrawal toward caregivers. When children suffer from this disorder, they rarely or only minimally seek comfort or respond to comfort when distressed. They also may have limited positive moods, rarely engage with others, and have episodes of otherwise unexplainable irritability, sadness, and fearfulness. Reactive attachment disorder can also develop after too many changes in caregivers and limited opportunities to bond with caregivers, as is often the case with children in the foster care system.[99]

By age 11, Anthony hated himself so much that he attempted suicide and was sent to a treatment facility, where he was once again abused, this time by a fellow patient. He believes this abuse happened not because his abuser—who was five years older than him—intended to abuse him, but because Anthony didn't know he was allowed to say no to sexual advances. "He wanted to be friends with me and to hold me and touch me and wanted me to touch him."

SOOTHING, SELF-REGULATION AND THE ROLE OF ATTACHMENT

Infants and children first develop their emotional regulation skills from their caregivers. In order to learn to self-regulate, infants must first experience what it feels like to be soothed by others.[90] Whether they are hungry, soiled, thirsty, gassy, scared, lonely or otherwise upset, when their needs are attended to, they become calm again. Soothing is achieved through being fed, changed, cuddled and nurtured by a trusted attachment figure.[91] Their own self-soothing skills develop through this process of being activated, reacting then being deactivated.

The ability to self-soothe or self-regulate is derived primarily from an infant's secure attachment to their caregiver.[92] When infants experience being soothed **at the appropriate time** and the soothing is **reliably, successfully and consistently provided,** they develop the ability to soothe themselves.[93] Those who are not reliably, successfully and consistently soothed may not develop self-soothing skills and will remain dysregulated.

Soothing not only protects children from the further effects of their immediately stressful situation, but it is also critical to their psycho-neurobiological development.[94] It is also foundational in developing their ability to 'attach' or to form healthy relationships with others later in life. Inconsistent love and support can cause attachment injuries.[95] (Attachment styles are discussed later.)The core of attachment is attunement, which is the special/distinct emotional bond that exists between an infant or toddler and their caregiver.[96]

If attachment does not exist or attachment figures are neglectful or abusive, or if they have difficulties self-regulating themselves, caregivers may negatively contribute to their children's emotional and physiological dysregulation.[97]

A child's emotional regulation skills continue to grow as they grow in the presence of their trusted attachment figures. Their skills develop through a process of activation and then deactivation. As children confidently experiment with their environment, by exploring it, their system becomes activated. After they experience distress, "Is this safe?" they look back to their caregiver to deactivate before venturing farther out, then eventually return home where they feel safe and soothed. As children mature, this ability and process extends itself into play and further experimentation with trusting others.[98]

One day a life changing event occurred. "It was a camp, and so we all had chores to do," explained Anthony. "He decided that I had to do all his chores, and when I said no, he just lit into me. So I ran out of the cottage."

One of the counselors came out after Anthony and told him it was okay that he had said no.

"He said, 'You know, you don't have to do anything you don't want to do.' [It] had such a profound effect on me. That night, when the kid came back and wanted to be in my bed, I said no."

THE RIGHT TO SAY NO

Victims who have been abused by one perpetrator often do not understand that they have a right to their own body or the right to say 'no'. As a result, they are often easy targets for further abuse.

Once Anthony learned he could say no, this abuse stopped. The sexual abuse perpetrated by his father ended shortly thereafter. "You know, the changes in my body, the hormones, something shifted. Somehow, now that I hit puberty, he was less interested in me that way."

AGING OUT

Offenders often lose interest in children when they "age out" and are no longer within the offenders' desired age of attraction.

Growing up, Anthony found therapy to be very helpful. "I have been in and out of treatment since I was 11. I've often turned to it throughout my life. I had a major depressive episode at 18 and went back into treatment.

That's when I discussed the camp incident, but in the context of having sex with another man. She [the therapist] did not label it as abuse. I was actually seeing her because I had a resurgence of suicidal thoughts. I wasn't eating and wasn't sleeping well at all. My father was not discussed."

It wasn't until years later that Anthony, then 37, told his therapist he did not bathe alone until after age 11. In response, his therapist blurted out, "Oh my, you were sexually abused by your father." Up until that point, Anthony didn't know that what he had endured in the bath was actually sexual abuse.

"I was very surprised, and she was very upset. She wanted to increase the number of sessions per week. She felt like it wasn't safe for me to continue therapy if I wasn't able to do it more frequently and so we terminated," Anthony said. "I don't know if any therapist was really prepared to deal with it [because] I didn't consider myself sexually abused. I didn't know what was happening between my father and me was sexual. To me, it was just bathing. There was nothing to disclose."

Anthony explained, "It's not like I was keeping it a secret, not like I was ashamed of it. I was not upset; I was confused. If you're beaten, that's aggressive. When you are supposedly being bathed, this was bathing!"

THE PROCESS OF NORMALIZATION

It is not uncommon for children to become normalized to wrongful sexual acts committed by a parent or trusted caregiver. They believe sexual acts are simply a normal part of everyday life since they have no point of reference for *normal*. The process begins when someone they trust introduces sexual acts into their relationship. Their abuser may tell them it is okay for them to do these things or that their relationship is "special." The devastation from these acts often manifests much later, in their teen years or beyond, when they learn that what happened was sexual abuse.

About one year later, Anthony's older sister disclosed to him that she had been sexually abused by their father. Anthony hadn't told her about his abuse. "Then she asked me if my father had abused me. Now that I had this information, I said yes. She asked me if it was while bathing. I again said yes." Anthony's sister was wrought with guilt and began apologizing profusely for not having protected him. She admitted that as a child she had suspected that when her father stopped abusing her, he had likely moved on to Anthony. Her apology made Anthony extremely uncomfortable. He told her that she didn't need to apologize, that his abuse wasn't her fault. She was only five years old at the time, and Anthony did not hold her responsible in any way, but this was not enough for her to console herself. Four months later, she committed suicide.

"I was very, very close to my older sister, and she was completely crushed by my admission, just crushed. I felt very, very guilty, horribly guilty. To this day, it causes me tremendous pain. I would not expect my five-year-old sister to protect me from my father. It's just not an issue for me. I'm not upset that she, at age five, was relieved that my father had moved on and left her alone."

After learning about his sister's abuse, Anthony decided to tell his younger sister since she now had children of her own. He disclosed his abuse but didn't share about his older sister's experience; he didn't feel it was his place to do this. Unfortunately, his younger sister didn't believe him. "She was extremely angry with me." Their relationship came to an end. "We have no relationship now. To her credit, she has never allowed my father to be alone with her children."

Around age 50, Anthony experienced another major depressive episode and reentered therapy. He went on psychotropic medications and for the first time focused on healing from his sexual abuse. Anthony now understands that the years of abuse he endured did substantial long-term damage and caused him to develop a personality disorder known as dissociative identity disorder, which was previously known as multiple personality disorder.

DISSOCIATIVE IDENTITY DISORDER (DID)

Dissociative identity disorder involves the development of one or more distinct "alters." These alters are secondary personalities that develop subconsciously, without the victim's awareness, to help them manage traumatic experiences like childhood abuse. One alter is often not aware of the others. Individuals with dissociative identity disorder often discover their alters when they emerge from an altered state and realize they are doing something that is completely outside of their usual character, such as finding evidence of smoking a cigarette when they don't smoke.

People with dissociative identity disorder sometimes have awareness of their alters and their unique characteristics. Anthony explained the discovery of his different alters, "I would get lost all the time. I would physically be in a space that I'd been in many, many times before, and I simply wouldn't recognize my surroundings or the names of the streets. I wouldn't know which way to turn because I was totally disoriented. I've been going to the same therapist for nine years, and I would walk into the room and say, 'When did you get that chair?' He'd say, 'I've had that chair for 15 years.' I'd just be amazed." Through these and other experiences, both Anthony and his therapist came to understand that he was struggling with dissociative identity disorder. They recognized that different alters were manifesting at different times.

For a decade prior to confronting his abuse, Anthony worked in the courts as a caseworker and was in frequent contact with children who had been similarly abused. As a trained therapist, he felt guilty, as if he should have been able to recognize his own abuse. Anthony's diagnosis helped him understand why he wasn't previously aware of his abuse, and it provided him with a context to understand other experiences that hadn't made sense in the past. He now attends group therapy and assists others who have dissociative identity disorder and who have survived sexual abuse.

"The confusion I live with and the confusion that people who care for me and relate to me live with, that's real. It's another aspect of being DID [dissociative identity disorder], the lack of connection. I can't explain it, nor the profound level of dissociation I've experienced," he said. "Periodically, new memories are released by whoever's keeping them from me. [My] awareness of the full extent of what happened to me all those years ago is becoming clearer and clearer."

Anthony's wife experiences some of his symptoms as her husband being purposefully "secretive." She can't relate and believes he is simply withholding information. Despite their challenges, Anthony is happily married, though he is pained that he never had children of his own.

"I just never thought I was healthy enough to be a parent, and that's a source of sadness for me," he said. "I do feel healthy enough to be a parent now, but of course, the means of parenthood are long behind me."

Despite his challenges Anthony has a successful career, and is very close to children in his network of extended family and friends. "I'm the person in the family that everyone comes to. If they're having a problem, they talk to me," he said. "They perceive me as calm, sensitive, and nonjudgmental, so I get called on."

Garrett: "I Knew Something was Wrong"

Garrett, 34, also believes that he was around two years old when his mother, a school teacher, began sexually abusing him. While he didn't discuss the details of the sexual abuse, he said that aside from being sexually abused by her, she also used him as her personal confidante. From a very early age, Garrett was *parentified* and forced to be his mother's surrogate spouse.

"I would have to go to these dinners and sit next to my mother. She just talked about my schooling and my report cards and I usually just wanted to die. I was more than a child; it was like I was her husband," he said. "These people thought that we were so close, and it was never a choice on my part to be close with her. It was kind of odd, this relationship with my mother, the way she'd relate to me. I didn't understand why she had this obsession with me. I knew it was very screwed up. She would always say, 'Oh, you're my favorite' or 'Oh, you're sensitive.' Yeah, I was sensitive because she trained me to be that way. I wanted to just run from my mother, but it was hopeless."

PARENTIFICATION

Parentification is a form of emotional (and often physical) abuse where children are made to play the role of a parent or caregiver. They are given developmentally inappropriate levels of responsibility, such as caring for their parent or other children in the family.

Garrett described his father as "a pretty scary guy." Although he was an esteemed professional, he "was always getting angry at someone and always threatening violence." Garrett's only other sibling was a younger brother, and Garrett believed that on some level he was protecting him from being the one to have screwed-up relationships with both of his parents. Although Garrett couldn't describe it, he knew something was very wrong. This experience of knowing something is wrong but not knowing how to describe it is common among victims of childhood sexual abuse.

Garrett's parents also controlled with whom, how, and where he spent his free time. "My mother was a teacher, so she was always super involved in everything. I wasn't really allowed to just have an experience. It was almost like she thought she could think for me. It felt really icky to hang out with my parents when I was an adolescent, but at some level they broke down my confidence to such an extent that I didn't really think that there was any way to escape."

Garrett was attractive, so girls often pursued him, but his mother would hang up on any girl who dared to call their house. Any time he managed to make progress toward having a friend of his own, his parents would interfere. Because of this interference, Garrett lacked friends and was left completely reliant on his parents for any sort of a social life.

"I desperately wanted to fit in, to just have people in my life who could understand where I was coming from. I think a lot of my attempts to relate to girls my age were actually my attempt to open up to someone." Garrett believes he was likely too intense in his own pursuits with friends and may have scared a few away.

In high school, Garrett began to see the hopelessness in his situation and threw himself into his studies. He aspired to someday create a better life for himself, and although he excelled both academically and athletically, inside he was deeply distressed. "I wanted a high school teacher to recognize that I was suicidal every day in high school. I got these glowing report cards, but I was almost doing that as a plea for help. I thought my parents were literally [going to] kill me if I didn't do well in school."

Garrett's teachers likely never suspected anything was wrong. He did well in school, and his parents put on a good front. "They presented this image of wholesome, decent, respectful people, but behind closed doors, I mean forget about it. It was very different. I think that's also why I wasn't vocal, because on some level they made me question my whole reality. 'Are they right and am I insane?'"

Garrett's parents also didn't allow him to set other personal boundaries. "Part of my abuse was I had to tell my mother way too much information so she could control me. They also didn't allow me to have part-time jobs. I would want to do some sort of work, and my dad would say, 'Oh, work's hard, go take care of your mother.' That was the role they put me in: take care of my mother. I hated that role."

There were many reasons Garrett didn't disclose his abuse early on. "First of all, it was a big risk." In his teens, Garrett was aware that things might not get any better for him if he were to be put in the care of the state. Then, in early adulthood, he also came to realize that he had no idea how to support himself. He knew he didn't know how to get a job and that he needed his parents' financial support to further his education.

Garrett doubted he could attend a university without his parents' help. Getting a student loan seemed unlikely given his parents' high earnings, plus his parents had conditioned him not to seek outside help. They'd taught him that any form of outside help was dangerous and futile, that the only people who really cared about him were his immediate family, and that everyone else would just be using him.

"My parents fostered this idea that I somehow was better than other people. I mean, at the core I knew it was all kind of false, and I felt dirty taking their money and going for expensive dinners, etc., but I also didn't want to give that up. Stepping outside of that felt almost impossible."

Also, disclosing the abuse "pretty much meant giving up everything that was familiar." Garrett's parents had raised him in an upper-class lifestyle, and he grew up with a strong sense of entitlement. In a sense, he wanted compensation for all he had been through. Garrett also didn't want to be responsible for breaking up his family, nor did he want to risk losing the opportunity to go to a university. "As screwed up [as it was], it was kind of the only thing I had at that point." Finally, Garrett also feared if he put an end to his abuse, his parents might begin abusing his brother.

When Garrett finally got to college, he began to establish friendships of his own. But "things just became more complicated. I was really off. I hadn't gone through these developmental steps of trying things out. Academically, I was at their level, but developmentally, it just became more accentuated, the difference." By the time he finished school, Garrett was ill-prepared for life on his own. "I was conditioned to be helpless. My parents wouldn't even let me pay my own bills in college. I never had that experience of figuring out how the world works."

When Garrett began working in corporate finance, things got significantly worse for him. He was required to report to a female marketing manager, and this activated his PTSD to the point that he became excessively dysregulated and physically unable to work.

"I knew something was wrong, but I didn't quite understand what. I could always do well in school and kind of perform the next task." Now he couldn't. "I couldn't conceptualize what the next step would be."

THE BODY REMEMBERS

In her 2000 book, *The Body Remembers: The Psychophysiology of Trauma and Trauma Treatment*, Babette Rothchild, LCSW, describes how victims' bodies remember and hold implicit memories of their trauma. These memories manifest and interfere later in life. Two common physiological responses based on remembering are **hypervigilance** and **hyperarousal**. Hypervigilance describes when a victim becomes hypersensitive to threats or potential threats. It generally involves the close monitoring of other people's hands, faces, words, emotions, and actions and planning escape routes. Upon perceiving threats, or something that reminds them of a threat, the victim will then become hyper-aroused. Hyperarousal is when bodily response suddenly kicks into high alert. The victims heart rate and respiration will increase and they may begin to sweat as a result of consciously or subconsciously remembering previous trauma.

At the time, he didn't know what was wrong. "I internalized that and said it must be because I am so off or don't have these skills. It must be a reflection of my worth as a person or something. It was definitely traumatizing."

Tragically, around this time, Garrett's closest friend was killed. "I was kind of a train wreck then." Confused by what was happening, he researched his symptoms online and sought therapy, assuming he most likely had PTSD. But even then, his mother interfered.

"[My] mother just hijacked the process. She would get in the way of me doing anything with the therapist." Garrett didn't understand why she would do this. "I mean, the last time I saw her, she was saying that I needed to go to therapy." He was disappointed the therapist allowed this to happen.

"These therapists who were supposedly trained would somehow send me the message that I wasn't [abused], to just get on with my life. Some of them said, 'Your family dynamics are maybe a little off,' but the message I took away was that I was somehow not strong enough or wasn't manly enough to just deal with everything."

When Garrett was 27, he began to sense that his issues may have been caused by sexual abuse, so he read the book *Victims No Longer: The Classic Guide for Men Recovering from Child Abuse* by psychotherapist Mike Lew. It was revelatory.

"It was the first time in my life that I felt someone was describing my experience. He described my inner reality throughout his book. It was simply by reading the book that I understood that I had been abused, that these symptoms that I had been presenting with were actually legitimate. I was just happy. I felt that there was someone in the world that had some idea of where I was coming from."

Garrett then found a therapist who specialized in working with male survivors of sexual abuse and came to understand himself better. He came to understand that he had been dissociating and that he had been conditioned to disconnect from his own thoughts and feelings. Once he understood better what was going on, he confronted his parents.

"They just denied everything. I got so angry that I wrote a letter to my mother, and I wrote a letter to her boss. I wanted to really hurt both my parents. After that, I was pretty much disowned from the family for bringing it into the public sphere. That was not allowed."

When Garrett reported his mother, his fears about losing their support came true. "[All] my fears in high school were really legitimate. If I had done that sooner, I might not have gotten through college." Although Garrett had hoped that his parents would admit their wrongs and validate his reality, possibly even continue to support him, he never got any positive response. Instead, he was banished from the family.

Garrett did get the validation and support he needed from his therapist, and he was further validated by all of the media attention surrounding the Jerry Sandusky case in 2011. But Garrett's case was complex. Diagnosed with complex PTSD and clinical depression, he came to understand that he too, had dissociative identity disorder. The condition could explain how he excelled academically during all his years of abuse. Garrett is aware of eight personalities—or "alters"—that handled his intense feelings which otherwise would have been too difficult for him to handle.

"A lot of the time I feel like I'm insane because people see me as a 34-year-old grown man. I can switch pretty quickly. Some of my alters are very young, and I just need to kind of comfort them and accept what they are feeling, which I have a real hard time with. I feel like I've betrayed them. Some are younger children and different genders. In the past, they've taken over, and I've acted in ways that people maybe don't understand."

In therapy, Garrett has worked on dialoguing with his alters, one of which is a four-year-old boy, and making sure he is taking care of them. "I'm doing much better. If I'm four-year-old little Jay, I can comfort him and accept him."

These days, Garrett leads a relatively normal life. He is a gentle, soft-spoken young man who coaches high school athletics. At the time of his interview, he was training to become a teacher and felt committed to providing his students with the support he never had. He hopes to establish a healthy romantic relationship with a woman.

Gordon: "My Dirty Little Secret"

Gordon, 38, grew up in a very small, rural, predominantly black and extremely religious southern community in what he described as 'the Bible Belt'. He was raised by his mother who held two, three and sometimes four jobs just to keep food on the table. Despite her efforts they often lived close, if not below, the poverty line and there were times when the only thing they could afford was creamed corn. For most of his youth it was just the two of them. Looking back, Gordon now recognizes they were enmeshed.

Gordon was abused multiple times by three people over eight years. Although he has few memories of his life before age 12, he knows his abuse began sometime around age five when his older stepbrother began forcing him to perform oral sex. Gordon grew up thinking it was his role or duty to satisfy the sexual needs of other people, and soon thereafter was "seduced" by an older male cousin and then again by a neighbor boy.

ENMESHMENT

Being enmeshed is where the parent-child relationship is simply too close. The child's boundaries are not respected and the child has difficulty escaping the parent or being autonomous. Although they may not be playing the role of parent or caregiver, the child is made to be more concerned with their parent's well-being than their own. For more information, check out two great books by clinical psychologists Dr. Kenneth Adams and Alexander Morgan, who specialize in the subject. The first is *Silently Seduced: When Parents Make Their Children Partners.* (Dr. Adams uses the term "covert incest" to describe relational patterns that are established separately from physical incest.) The second book is *When He's Married to Mom: How to Help Mother-Enmeshed Men Open Their Hearts to True Love and Commitment.*

"I was used as a sexual object. I was used to gratify their sexual needs. I remember a lot of role playing, like 'pretend to be this' and being told what to do. But because I was young, there was nothing done to me. As far as I know I was never anally assaulted. It was always oral, I was performing: oral sex, fellatio...things like that."

Gordon thought very little of being used like this because he knew of several other children in his community who were being similarly abused. Although none had ever openly discussed their abuse, "survivors just know other survivors," he said. Gordon said that sexual abuse was an unspoken and accepted part of their community.

"Mom would say, 'If some creepy old man grabs you, scream and yell and throw yourself on the ground.' But no one ever said if your uncle touches your penis or aunt puts her finger up your butt, scream, run, come tell somebody. No one ever said that. Never ever. The only people you worried about molesting you were the creepy guys driving the van."

Gordon didn't remember how or why his abuse ended, only that it stopped when he was 11 or 12. He remained silent for several years in part to protect himself and others in his extended family who lived nearby. Their family had a strong public image that had been cultivated over many generations.

"Nobody could see that the family members would be the perpetrator even though the perpetrators were all around us. It was familial, an [incestuous] thing. I can name on one hand the people [who] lived in my general area [who] sustained child abuse and to this day still haven't discussed it. We all knew about it as kids. We all saw the signs, but no one talked about it. It wasn't talked about in school."

Gordon feared that if he spoke up about his abuse, there would be consequences not only for his family but for the entire community. So he remained silent and instead maintained the illusion of being a model kid. "I didn't cuss, didn't drink, didn't smoke, didn't go with girls. I was very strong. I was the leader of our youth group. I mean you couldn't even *pour* alcohol on me."

In his late teens things changed. Gordon began living a promiscuous and addictive lifestyle. He started drinking heavily, having lots of sex, and kept himself so busy with work that even on weekends he had little time to reflect on what had happened earlier in his life. He remained silent about his abuse initially because, like many other men, Gordon hadn't viewed what had taken place as abuse. Also, he reasoned that if sex itself was a taboo topic in his community, it must be worse to talk about sexual abuse.

As an adult, Gordon remained silent about the abuse he had experienced in part because there were no resources for males, and because he was confused about his sexuality. He was attracted to men but didn't know why. Few other men in his southern community in the mid-1990s were openly gay.

"Back then, being homosexual was against societal norms and it wasn't something people ever discussed," he said. "It was something that you found in the back of tabloid magazines or you just knew of that certain street that you could go cruise. There were barely two gay bars in the whole state. If you thought that someone was gay, that was just Uncle So-and-So, that's just how he is or that's his friend, but it just wasn't talked about. Things like that were just unspoken. It was the same thing with sexual abuse." No one spoke of sexual orientation either. Even as an adult, he was wrapped up in being what he considered "a good Southern Baptist."

Gordon also had significant memory loss issues, which meant he wasn't bothered by intrusive memories at first. He recalls very little of his life between age five and 12. "I'll look at family pictures and have no recollection. I had a pony when I was little. I mean, what eight-year-old kid wouldn't remember their pony? There's a picture of me sitting on a pony with a pony cart and everything. I don't remember Christmas. I don't remember birthdays." Gordon believes there is still much more that he has yet to remember.

MEMORY LOSS

Memory loss is common among trauma survivors. More than half of the men I interviewed reported retaining only a partial memory or no memory at all of their abuse, at least for a period of time. Although many buried their memories without any conscious effort, some made a conscious decision to try and forget what had happened and were successful for many years. Memory loss and dissociation are common responses to trauma.[100]

Gordon married but then began experiencing a dark depression. He began therapy, divorced, ended his therapy, and began it again after his second marriage also ended badly. He explained that after being abused by so many men and coming to believe that it was his duty to appease them, he had a hard time engaging with women sexually. "I have to be almost seduced, and I can't just have a one-night stand because I'll completely dissociate and go into a work mode," he said. "I'll perform."

Gordon now sees a trauma therapist whom he says has seen "the worst of the worst." He is able to openly discuss his abuse and is back in touch with his faith. Like two of the other men interviewed, Gordon was also diagnosed with dissociative identity disorder. He too, found his diagnosis useful because it helped him begin to make sense of certain experiences after one of his alters had been active. For example, at work a supervisor once asked why he was there on his day off. Gordon didn't remember asking for days off or being granted them. He came to understand that one of his alters must have put in the request.

"I'd never had problems with memory before. I never lose anything," he said. "All of a sudden things were disappearing."

He described his diagnosis as comforting "but also very bizarre." He explained that his process of "discovering" his alters was like "getting to know new people and making new friendships." One of his alters watches pornography and is very sexually promiscuous. Others are children. One is a gatekeeper.

Gordon didn't tell his mother about his abuse until his mid-twenties, well after she had remarried and was more financially stable. He waited until she had someone to take care of her and until she could see that he was now safe from his abusers. He still has not disclosed his abusers' identities, nor does he plan to until after his grandmother has passed away. "I'm protecting her. I will let her go to her grave believing her family is intact."

Gordon works at a crisis center and as a youth educator, but finds the work somewhat frustrating because he's prohibited from discussing anything except abstinence with youth. "We are still backwards in many, many ways. We do talk about sexual assault in our program, but we have to be very careful when we answer the questions."

Josh: "I Thought It Was My Fault"

Josh, 48, was raised in a tight-knit family that held traditional views regarding respect for elders and family loyalty. He also grew up knowing he had been an unplanned child and that his arrival had created financial hardship for the family.

"I was reminded that the family never drank orange juice before I was born. When I came along, orange juice was brought in because I always had colds or strep throat or something like that. This orange juice was looked upon as a luxury item. I mean it might as well have been champagne. My perception of their view back then was that I was spoiled. I was the youngest brother and among the youngest cousins. I felt very isolated and very alone as a child."

When they were away, Josh's parents often left him in the care of two older female cousins who didn't treat him very well. Initially, they would just do things like unplug the TV and tell him it had stopped working. But when he was seven their abusive behaviors turned exploitive as they took advantage of his innocence and sexually abused him.

The abuse occurred one day when Josh's parents were away visiting his godparents. He was left alone with his two cousins. They were playing pool when Josh made an offhand comment about not knowing what girls looked like. His cousins shamed him for being naïve, coerced him to look at them, and then to perform oral sex on each of them. The experience was both terrifying and humiliating for Josh, but he didn't disclose the incident to his parents because they had previously instilled in him the message that "if it happens to you, it is likely your fault." In this case, Josh thought it was his fault because he'd made a comment about not knowing what girls looked like.

A few years later, when Josh was 10 years old he was abused again. This time it was by an older male cousin who was eight years his senior. This cousin had offered to teach Josh how to play a game, which he later understood was strip poker. During the game, when Josh expressed discomfort, his cousin criticized him for having said he wanted to play a game but then not wanting to play. He then instructed Josh to fellate him and attempted to sodomize him. He may have been successful had another cousin not come to the door. When she knocked Josh instinctively dressed himself very quickly. He knew that what they had been doing was wrong, but didn't tell anyone because he didn't want to get in trouble or cause problems within the family.

In high school Josh recognized that he was attracted to men, and he fell deeply in love with his best friend. When that friend asked him to have sex, Josh turned him down out of loyalty to his parents. He knew they were strongly opposed to homosexuality, and he'd learned not to breach familial loyalties or boundaries out of fear of being disowned. He had seen it happen to other family members.

"My uncle decided to divorce and then all of a sudden we weren't supposed to like Aunt Saundra. I learned the lesson that family loyalty was absolutely important."

Josh also learned it was his job to keep family secrets and that his father had anger issues. "Since age six, we'd been doing everything very gently, tip-toeing around him. He never addressed us directly, but his message was clear: 'I don't want to talk about it.' So I separated my family out from the rest of what I call my 'real life.'"

As a means of survival, Josh taught himself to simply pretend that everything was wonderful. He carried on the act until it became his truth, and he literally forgot that his assaults had ever occurred.

"It was like I have to put this out of my mind. I have to pretend it never happened. It was as if I were physically pushing something away," he said. "It was as if [taking his water glass and pushing it out of his line of sight] I don't want to see this glass anymore. I don't want to look at it, I can't look at this glass anymore, I can't, I can't, I can't, I can't, 'til I can't see the glass anymore. Okay, I can't see the glass [a sigh of relief]."

In his freshman year of college, Josh, who now identified as bisexual, was severely hazed and he began to feel very alone and very troubled.

"I felt like my life was a waste, like there was an undercurrent in my life, but I didn't know what was pulling me under."

Although Josh began therapy and was diagnosed with depression, his therapy wasn't helping. He was still distressed but his memories of abuse were repressed.

THOUGHT SUPPRESSION

Many victims have intrusive thoughts or reminders of the traumatic events they have experienced. Since these thoughts are upsetting, victims often make conscious attempts to suppress them.[101] While helpful in the short term, thought suppression can actually result in an increase in the frequency and intensity of the thoughts they are trying to avoid.[102] Although some are successful at burying their memories, the memories don't always stay buried. Suppressed memories can resurface later in life when they finally feel safe enough to deal with them. The resurfacing of traumatic memories can be very disruptive. Aside from those who purposefully try to forget their abuse, a greater number of people identify their memory loss as an automatic, subconscious process. Their brains simply protect them from information that is too hard for them to handle at the time. The men in this research each believe their involuntary memory loss occurred as an adaptive physiological response to the trauma they experienced, which would have otherwise been intolerable.

"I had nothing left to talk to my therapist about except my abuse. I had worked through every single issue with him and my therapist was frustrated because I was not making progress."

Josh's therapist asked him if he had ever been sexually abused. He responded with 'no' because at that point he still didn't remember. "I absolutely did not recall. I honestly believed I hadn't been abused."

Josh remembers struggling to understand why he had made very little progress after six years of therapy. He frequently awoke in a state of panic in the middle of the night, but had no idea what he was afraid of. "I was scared shitless. I would walk around my apartment and do anything I could to calm myself down." But it was to no avail. He remained unsettled and retreated further and further into himself. He even contemplated suicide.

When Josh was in his mid-thirties he was sexually assaulted for a third time. By then he was working for the Peace Corps in Africa. One night while Josh was on vacation, travelling around Africa staying in different Peace Corp offices, a volunteer coordinator invited Josh to stay with him and another visiting superior. Josh recognized that the fellow visitor was gay but he didn't think much about it. The three spent the evening enjoying each other's company, drinking and smoking marijuana. Josh got very high then headed off to bed alone. He had fallen asleep when the visiting superior came into his bed and began to fondle him. "He basically just started having sex with me," Josh said. "He came in and started kissing and fondling me." Josh wasn't interested in having sex and attempted to stop his assailant, but the man persisted. Even though he was an adult Josh felt powerless to stop him.

"I was like, he needs to get out of my bed, but I had no voice for this kind of thing. I wasn't remembering my past." Josh recalled thinking that if he could just make the man orgasm he would stop. "I basically gave him a hand job until he came, but then I just kept pumping 'cause I knew it would be painful afterwards. He was like, 'Stop, that hurts.' He wanted to masturbate me but I told him 'no' and he left." Josh stated that "he slept peacefully, and I stayed up most the night feeling dirty and disgusting."

CONSENT

Children are never able to consent to sexual acts. For adults to consent to sexual acts, both participants must be conscious and mentally capable of consenting. There is a great YouTube video called *Tea Consent* by Blue Seat Studios that discusses what true consent looks like. They use the parallel of offering someone a cup of hot tea. You don't just pour it on them if they aren't awake or if they tell you they don't want tea. (Warning: Adult language.)

Josh believes the assault was planned in advance. The next day, he felt like he couldn't complain because of who and where he was. Josh was openly gay/bisexual and travelling alone in a country where homosexuality was a crime. He worried that if he complained he wouldn't be welcome back in the office. He knew he might need them as a resource if he got into trouble.

"That's exactly what I thought: I won't be invited back." He also thought it was partly his own fault, "like I invited it on myself for being such a fag. So I just decided to throw that one under the carpet. It just became another thing."

He was also aware of the bigger picture. "I could have asked to speak to the medical officer and made a complaint, but here we are in Africa where life is tough. I mean white people coming from the outside, their life is automatically posh. We don't have problems. How could I disrespect the culture by complaining about something?"

As a result, Josh reasoned, "I was like, okay, I wasn't killed, he didn't maim me, he didn't do anything to me. I went through with the rest of my trip and had a great vacation! I toughed it out. So it included sexual assault! I made it through. I can take care of myself no matter how miserable I am."

A few years later, the memories of his earlier childhood abuse came back.

"I don't know if I had watched a repeat of *Oprah* or a documentary on male survivors of sexual abuse, but I can tell you something just shook loose. I was sitting in my apartment and I was like, 'Wow, I remember this. This really happened. Why have I not been thinking about this all these years? Why have I not put all of this together?' I was knocking my head, figuratively, against the wall."

After recovering his memory, Josh decided it was time to tell his friends, but most of them told him that they already knew, that he'd told them about it already. Josh didn't remember this.

"It was a convenient blank slate," he said. "What would happen is that every now and then, it would force its way into my consciousness. I might tell somebody and then it would disappear. I swear to you it would disappear. I would repress the memory."

Josh believes all of his memories have now returned to him. He has been able to integrate and process these memories with the help of his therapist. Josh has now been diagnosed with PTSD. He has told his family about the abuse and is now in good mental health. He currently works as the head of a department at a respected university in the United States.

Leon: "I Didn't Remember"

Leon was 58 when he shared the "unique and complicated" aspects of his abuse and recovery story. He explained that although he was not consciously aware of it, he had used alcohol to numb himself from the emotional pain associated with his abuse. Through the use of alcohol, he too, was successful at temporarily burying the memories of his abuse, which began when he was 13.

The year after Leon's father died, his mother, then 38 and still grieving and lonely, befriended a young school teacher named Scott.

"I don't have any recollection of how they met, but he was about 29 and still living at home. He would come over and they would drink and smoke cigarettes and talk. I believe they had a platonic relationship," Leon said. "I was around and my younger sister was around too. She was three years younger. He became a friend of the family."

Scott wasn't Leon's teacher, so when he offered to be Leon's friend and role model, his mother accepted. He took Leon on outings and paid special attention to him. Leon, who missed his father, welcomed the attention. During the Christmas holidays, when Scott's parents went out of town, he took Leon to his own house. "I don't remember how he got me there, only that it was cold outside and that the house was dimly lit with yuletide decorations." Scott introduced Leon to alcohol.

"It was hard liquor, and one thing led to another. He moved on to touching and caressing me, and we wound up in the master bedroom where he raped me anally."

This abusive relationship continued for a while. "I know there was oral sex involved. A lot of it was in the car," Leon recalled.

Shortly after, Leon also began being abused by a second man, a priest who was in his early sixties and was Scott's "special friend."

"He was not violent and not as aggressive. It was very gradual, much more touching and caressing, masturbating, that sort of thing. That lasted a couple years on and off."

Although he didn't like the interactions, Leon didn't understand that what was happening was abuse. At the time he felt trapped and powerless to stop it. He also felt obligated to please these two men, who paid him special attention at a time when he desperately needed it. Both of these abusive relationships lasted until Leon was 17 years old.

After, Leon went on to lead a somewhat normal life. He got married, raised four children, and served as the chief executive officer of a large corporation. However, despite appearances, Leon hid a secret from the people in his immediate circle. His secret was not the abuse but that he had drunk alcohol daily from the first time he was introduced to it by his abuser at age 13.

No one knew the extent of his alcoholism for 35 years, not his wife, boss, or any of his friends or staff. Leon never understood his strong desire to drink, and only ever briefly reflected on his years of abuse. He believes the alcohol consumption protected him from the pain of acknowledging what he had been through.

"Alcohol removed me from the world in many ways and numbed me to my feelings. It also protected me from dealing with the pain until I was ready. There was this self-forgetting, if you will, that just perpetuated itself and kept it all buried. I buried the abuse for 35 years. It was almost like a protective mechanism. Obviously, there were times when I reflected on it, but it just never was front and center enough that I wanted to pay attention to it. On top of consciously not thinking about it, there was a deep unconscious thing going on. It just got buried, and life just kept on going.

"The alcohol removed me from the pain of ever dealing with it and what impact it may have had on my life. It was almost as if God contributed to my keeping it buried all those years, you know, saying, 'We're going to wait. You're too good of a person. We need you around. We need to wait for you to deal with this.' I never actually forgot everything; there were always a couple of incidents that were pretty clear in my mind. I would have nightmares about something and they'd kind of form into memories."

Although Leon repressed most of the memories of his abuse, his body never forgot what had happened and dealt with it in a very unique way. At the age of 47, after a particularly heavy night of drinking, Leon was arrested for driving under the influence of alcohol and faced losing his driver's license for a second time. He was frightened and decided to stop drinking that night. (Quitting drinking abruptly like this is not recommended. It can cause considerable disruption to your system which may be dependent on alcohol. If you are going to stop drinking, do so with a physician's support.) After 35 years of daily alcohol use Leon experienced considerable withdrawal symptoms in the days that followed, and he began to feel suicidal.

"One day I was in my office after hours and I was literally spinning like a top, falling down, crawling around like a baby, and I somehow managed to call my [Alcoholics Anonymous] sponsor. I told him I was feeling suicidal," Leon said. "His response was, 'Look, this is out of my league, go to the ER, and I'll meet you there.'"

Leon took his advice and went to the hospital where he was admitted to the closed psychiatric unit for an eight-day psychiatric assessment. While on the unit, Leon began experiencing a peculiar limp in his right leg. In outpatient rehab, his limp became more and more pronounced, to the point that he began falling down and having difficulty walking. After any kind of physical injury was ruled out, Leon was referred to a psychologist, a psychiatrist, and a neurologist and was prescribed 11 different psychotropic medications. He had MRIs and saw numerous specialists, but nothing cured his limp.

As time went on, Leon grew more and more depressed and began to experience more pain in his leg. He even felt pain in his penis. Leon compared himself to the hunchback of Notre Dame, exhausted and in pain.

Leon was referred to a top neurologist who was an expert in dealing with conversion disorders. This doctor asked Leon to walk a corridor that would take the average person about one minute to cover. It took Leon 20 minutes. The neurologist confirmed that both the limp and the pain he was experiencing were real, that Leon was not faking his symptoms. He also explained to Leon that although he was experiencing symptoms, there was nothing wrong with him physically, though something was very wrong with him psychologically. He suggested it might be something Leon had buried or never talked about that had caused him to develop a somatic symptom disorder (previously known as a somatoform disorder)—a type of conversion disorder.

SOMATIC SYMPTOM DISORDERS/CONVERSION DISORDERS

Some physical disorders are believed to be a result of psychological distress or mental illness that manifests in a physiological manner. Patients with these disorders experience one or more persistent symptoms, which are distressing and disruptive to their daily life but have an otherwise unexplainable origin (after proper medical examination and testing). These symptoms may include pain, gastrointestinal distress, numbness, and sexual dysfunction. Conversion disorders are somatic symptom disorders marked by persistent symptoms that include a loss of function.

Leon was sent to a psychiatrist who also specialized in conversion disorders, and the two set the goal of trying to uncover what it was that Leon had buried. For the next several months, they combed through the details of his upbringing and early life experiences. They hadn't yet discussed his teen years when Leon's memories returned one day while he was out walking with his

Alcoholics Anonymous sponsor. The two were discussing the work Leon was doing with his psychiatrist, and exchanging stories about their past, when Leon's sponsor asked him about the first time he ever had a drink.

It wasn't something Leon had thought about in a long time, and the question stopped him in his tracks. He fell to his knees and began to weep as the memories of his first drink with his abuser came flooding back. Leon believes his intense therapy, supportive sponsor, and sobriety finally enabled him to uncover what he had repressed for more than 35 years. Leon believes that he finally felt safe enough to allow the memories to surface.

Leon recalled the emotional intensity, confusion, and disorientation that he'd felt during his abuse experience—the same feelings that led him to use alcohol in the first place. Leon also felt confused about his sexuality. He'd been aroused by two different men and had developed a genuine affection for both of his abusers. His young, grieving mind had failed to recognize that what these two men had done to him was grooming and abuse. As an adult, he had not yet made the connection between his alcoholism, somatoform disorder, and experience of abuse. Shortly after making the connection and processing his abuse memories Leon's limp went away and never returned.

Phillip: "It Never Occurred to Me that I Should Tell"

Phillip, 82, a gentle giant of a man, said that the sexual abuse he experienced at the hands of his father was actually only a minor part of his abuse story. He had grown up in a very physically and emotionally abusive family. Phillip believes his emotional abuse began the day he was born because his father, a Methodist minister, already had his entire life planned out for him.

"I was supposed to relive my father's life for him," Phillip said. "My father had my entire life planned for me and he controlled my life completely."

Despite the fact that his father was a minister, Phillip had seen him "go off" on people. Plus, at home his father was a very angry, passive-aggressive, judgmental, and controlling man. His mother wasn't much better. She was mentally ill and used Phillip as her full-time caregiver. "I was her emotional support. I was her caretaker rather than her being mine. She always told me that I was the best son a mother ever had." However, she rarely exhibited any affection toward Phillip.

As a result of his mother's lack of affection and his father's control and aggression, Phillip grew up feeling like an orphan, unloved and unnurtured. He recalls that he was not emotionally attached to either of his parents. When Phillip was five or six years old, he went for a long walk around a large lake where they lived. The police eventually found him and took him home, where his father scolded him for upsetting his mother. From that point on, Phillip's mother began tying him up in the backyard.

"So I didn't wander away, she'd tie a rope around my waist and tied it to the back of the house. I remember sort of cowering and hiding down in the corner trying to hide from my playmates so the other kids in the neighborhood didn't see me tied up like a dog."

In public and in his church community, Phillip saw his father maintain the façade of being a pillar of the community, but at home he was a very different man. Although he didn't actually beat Phillip, he threatened physical violence if Phillip failed to comply with his demands. He chose Phillip's clothes, the sports he played, and even whom he was allowed to date. He also told Phillip what he was going to be when he grew up: a doctor. His father's plan was that Phillip would attend an Ivy League university (paid for via a football scholarship), become a doctor, and play professional football. It didn't matter to him that Phillip had no interest in practicing medicine.

When Phillip was 14 years old, his father began anally raping him. A while later he also sent him to spend the weekend with his "friend."

"I always say he pimped me out! I was supposed to spend the whole weekend with this man, and after one night I just left. I was really afraid that my father was going to come down on me for having left his friend, but he never said a word. I'm pretty sure he was having sexual relations with him as well."

After being raped by his father for the fourth or fifth time, Phillip mustered up the courage to challenge him physically and the abuse ended. "He

[came] into my bedroom in the morning and I just picked him up and set him down in the corner of the room. I went back to bed, and that was the end of it."

Phillip didn't speak to anyone about his abuse for years. He suffered depression and suicidal thoughts, but felt too ashamed to say anything. During this time of suffering he was bothered by two recurrent nightmares.

"I don't remember when they started, but in both I am younger than when the abuse occurred," he said. "One was in the bedroom; this big black cloud would fill the bedroom. It would roll over me, engulf me, and suffocate me. The other was … we had a hallway with stairs going up. The ceiling was two stories high. It was really bizarre. I would be flying, hovering up in the hallway, and there'd be somebody on the stairway trying to get hold of me. I would be beginning to tire and they would get hold of me."

NIGHTMARES

Nightmares are common among victims of trauma and can make falling asleep very difficult or feel very unsafe. Many trauma victims stay up late trying to avoid nightmares. Unfortunately, this can snowball since lack of sleep affects a person in every area of life. If you suffer from nightmares, there's a great book called *No More Nightmares: How to Use Planned Dream Intervention to End Nightmares* by Dr. Beverly Ann Dexter that may help. The protocol is easy to understand and implement.

Like many others, Phillip eventually repressed the memories of his abuse until much later in life. He did so partly because he knew that he couldn't talk about it with anyone, and partly because it never occurred to him that he should. His abuse occurred in the 1940s, when it seemed nobody spoke of sexual abuse.

"It never occurred to me that I should tell or that it was a criminal act or anything. It was a whole lockdown situation for whatever reason, probably more shame than anything else," said Phillip.

Phillip's brain protected him. "The subconscious says, 'Well, you're not ready to deal with this, I'm going to hold it down here for a while. I'm going to keep it hidden from you until the time comes when you can deal with it.'"

After leaving home Phillip rebelled against his father. Instead of going the Ivy League route, he attended a small but reputable college and then allowed himself to flunk out.

"I didn't actually study. I wound up spending three years in the army. I think that was my way of telling him no, that I wasn't gonna study medicine. In my family you couldn't actually say no, you couldn't ask for what you wanted. The only way you could get anything was to be passive-aggressive and eventually hope they caved."

After getting kicked out of school Phillip joined the military, and later obtained his PhD in science. He became very successful in his career as a scientist, but that wasn't what his father had wanted.

"My father was not happy," Phillip said. "I had an international reputation, but it was not good enough. So that's the kind of person he was."

Phillip married and had children of his own, but he suffered with depression and suicidal thoughts for many years. He continued to have those same two nightmares well into his seventies when he finally began his recovery. Phillip had started going to Al-Anon because one of his stepsons struggled with a heroin and cocaine addiction. It was there that he began to see some behaviors in himself that he didn't like. He recognized his own inappropriate anger, fear, suspicious nature, and passive-aggressive behaviors.

"If someone was nice to me, I wondered what they wanted from me. I was just afraid of people, that sort of thing. Then I began to wonder where these behaviors had come from. I thought well, you know, probably family of origin, so I found a therapist who specialized in family of origin work to go back and see where these attitudes and behaviors were coming from.

There was a lot of talk about my father, and one day the therapist just asked me, 'Were you ever sexually abused by your father?' and all of the memories came flooding back. I could see the room, I could see him, I could see the sunshine, and I could see myself, you know, lying on the bed and wondering, 'Where the hell is my mother?' I also clearly remembered being with the other man."

"I asked him [the therapist], 'Why did you ask me that question?' I assumed it was because I was displaying characteristics of somebody who had been abused. He said no, it was because there was something creepy about my father."

By this time Phillip's father had died.

"The therapist said that I couldn't have done this work while my father was still alive because my father had too much control over me. Maybe that had some impact on my repressing it, his control. The decision to forget was not mine. I buried it completely. It never rose to the conscious level for 45 years. I just repressed it. I guess it was something that was just intolerable that my conscious mind didn't want to deal with, I don't know. I always say that your subconscious only allows things to come up that you can deal with, and a little at a time."

Phillip was stunned. He went home, told his wife, and began to look for other support and resources. He disclosed his abuse publicly during a Take Back the Night candlelight vigil where he was interviewed by a television reporter who asked him why he was there, since he was one of the only men in the crowd.

"I said, 'To support people who have been sexually abused' and then something else about men need help to disclose and get help too.' He said it would be on the news, and it was—my name and all. No one said a word. We never heard anything from anybody."

Phillip eventually joined a group for adults who had been molested as children, and again he was the only man. He also took the mandatory train-ing to volunteer at a local rape recovery center, where he worked on a crisis line for the next several years. Throughout this process, Phillip experienced healing and support, but the most dramatic healing took place when he attended a weekend of recovery event hosted by MaleSurvivor.org.

Phillip is now part of a group for adult male survivors of childhood sexual abuse.

"I don't know why my father did [what he did]. I'd love to talk to him, but all this didn't come to light until after he'd died. He would have lied to me anyway, but I would have the satisfaction of saying, 'You son of a b*tch.'"

Leonard: "Why Do You Hate Your Mother so Much?"

Leonard, 39, described himself as a shy, gentle child. He said that he was about four when his mother began physically and sexually abusing him. Soon after, she also began allowing her male friend to abuse him. Leonard's father, an alcoholic, worked out of town during the week and stayed away every other weekend. While he was gone, Leonard's mother and her friend, Sam, drank and hosted orgies upstairs while Leonard and his brother were downstairs. Leonard never told his father. He was already emotionally unavailable and Leonard didn't want to jeopardize what little relationship they had.

"I was fairly certain he knew I was being beaten, but I don't think he knew about the sexual abuse," Leonard said. "I have since learned he definitely knew about my mother's affair."

Although he was a gentle and shy kid, Leonard didn't have many real friends. He was considered the weird kid and got teased a lot. "Growing up in a hick town, if you are not a hockey player, you are a nobody." Leonard preferred to spend time alone, usually in the woods, reading or building a tree fort. He didn't play any sports.

At first, Leonard didn't understand that anything was wrong at home, but he avoided being there as much as possible. He didn't like the abuse, though at the time, he didn't know that's what it was. He spent most of his time alone or next door with his paternal grandparents. "If it wasn't for them,

I'd probably be completely insane," he said. Although he never disclosed his abuse to them, he took comfort in their otherwise close relationship and tried to live a normal life. Leonard went to church with his grandparents, sang in the choir, and even made plans to become a minister.

"My grandfather would have believed me, but at that time he was already on heart attack number eight or nine. I certainly didn't want to aggravate that, and my grandmother would not have understood."

Around 11, Leonard developed the physical strength and courage to challenge his mother, and the abuse ended.

"I don't know whether it was maturity or stories or what that made me realize it was wrong, but I put a stop to it myself," he recalled. "I think she'd asked me to bring beer up for her and Sam. That was not unusual. They were up in the bedroom, and I was downstairs watching TV. My brother was away on a ski trip with the school. I stood at the bottom of the stairs and threw two unopened bottles up the stairs, and they smashed at the top of the stairs. She came down and proceeded to beat the living crap out of me, but I just started laughing and said, 'You can't hurt me anymore,' and that was it. I'm pretty sure she was scared, because at that point she realized that I could go to the police or tell somebody or something."

By 12, Leonard had become fearless and angry and wanted to get his mother in trouble. He wasn't ready to talk about his abuse, so he went to his teacher and told her about a lesser concern, which was his mother's affair. He did this in hopes that it would start enough gossip so that his mother would either lose or be forced to leave her job. His parents had separated, and he reasoned that if his mom were to be humiliated enough, she would send him to live with his father. Instead, Leonard's teacher called his mother, and when he got home, she beat him. After that, Leonard didn't trust anybody for a very long time, and he was deterred from seeking anyone else's help.

Leonard had other reasons for not disclosing at this stage in his life. He didn't want people to treat him differently; plus, he'd read that most sex offenders had been abused themselves. He didn't want people thinking he might grow up to become a pedophile himself.

"There was still a lot of information out there that suggested that most pedophiles were abused," he said. "That was terrifying."

By age 12, Leonard had begun to direct a lot of his anger toward God. He couldn't understand how a loving God would allow abuse to occur, let alone to someone so devoted to Him. He assumed it was God's will, left the church, and developed an interest in dark poetry, heavy metal music, drugs, and alcohol. Around age 15, Leonard recognized these same interests in a female friend of his older brother and sensed that she too, had been abused. One night when they were drinking together, he decided to disclose his abuse. He "needed to get it out somehow so [he] didn't implode."

"I don't know if it's common among people that have been abused in general, but we always seem to find other people that have been abused. You read the signs with how they act, and it just comes up. We were both just sort of dark and twisty, heavy into dark poetry and literature and heavy metal music. We both smoked a lot of drugs, and we were just generally angry people, and we connected over being angry."

Once Leonard started the conversation, his friend followed suit and the two teens had an open discussion about their abuse experiences. Soon after, Leonard began to tell his other friends. He wanted people to understand him, and he knew they couldn't unless they knew about his past.

"I told because I'd get drunk and have violent outbursts or because they'd ask, 'Why do you hate your mother so much?' Sometimes I'd just blurted out the truth to shut them up. I might've been in a bad mood or feeling jealous that they had a mother. You know, any number of things. With friends, they generally expect that you will talk about your mom. You go for dinner, you know, questions come up. Like, 'Why did you write that song? What's going on?'"

"I don't know if having a death wish is the right way to put it, but I was fearless. I would jump over a six-foot bonfire whether I got burned or not! I told my girlfriend in particular, because I had nightmares. I'd wake up screaming, and my sexual appetite was sometimes higher than [my girlfriends] were expecting. I would go through these weird phases where it would be like 'don't touch me,' then the next day that's all [I] would want. I am assuming that is different for everybody; for me, it has a lot to do with the PTSD."

By the time Leonard was 19 or 20, he was ready to go to the police. He asked his older brother, who had also been abused by their mother, to go with him, but he refused. He told Leonard, "I'm not talking about it."

"I was ready to tell the world and try to put my mother in jail. My brother told me that if I went to the police that I was on my own. He told me, 'You're going to f*** up everything, don't say anything.'"

Leonard's brother didn't want anyone to know what was happening at home, and Leonard didn't want to deal with this alone so he didn't. "Between my dad [being unavailable] and my brother's unwillingness to cooperate, I just didn't think it was [something] I wanted to go through on my own." About a year later, when Leonard was 21, his father stopped drinking and pursued a closer relationship with him. Despite their closer relationship, Leonard still didn't disclose his abuse because he feared his father might start drinking again. Drinking had already significantly impacted his health. "It was bad enough that I didn't have a mother. I finally had a relationship with him. He finally started to become the father he had never been. We were still at that point of pretending that everything was normal," he said.

Leonard worried the truth might drive his father back to drinking and actually kill him, and he didn't want to take that risk.

A while after Leonard became a father himself, he made the decision to confront his mother and report the abuse to the authorities. His daughter was a few years old, and he hadn't had any contact with his parents, apart from the occasional phone call with his father, in years. After his son was born, Leonard's older brother moved his family to live closer to Leonard's.

Their move brought his parents back into the picture since his brother was still allowing their mother access to his children.

Leonard realized and feared that if both he and his wife died, his brother might gain custody of his children. If that happened, his brother would likely allow their mother access to his children.

"It dawned on me that I needed to protect my kids, and the only way to do that was to tell the truth."

Before going to the police, Leonard sent an email to his father informing him about the abuse and his intentions of reporting his mother. "It was kind of like, hey dad, heads up. This is the story. I am sorry you had to find out this way, but I am on the way to the police station."

The moment he hit send, he headed down to the police station. Later, he went and confronted his mother. He told her that if she cooperated by telling the truth and providing details about the abuse and her co-abuser, that he would not press charges against her personally. He would only pursue her friend, Sam.

"I don't know why I was willing to be lenient towards her, except that I had always felt, for no particular reason, that he had sort of talked her into it, brainwashed her. Also, he was going to be more difficult to get to. I had no ties to him. Even though she was still in contact with him and they were still friends, I had no way of making him pay, so I was trying to convince my mother to come with me to the police so we could at least put him behind bars. I also told her flat out, 'You will be a registered sex offender or there is no deal.'"

Leonard's mother refused his offer.

"She told me that I didn't understand and that there [were] a lot of things I didn't know. She didn't tell me what those things were. She tried to play the 'I've asked for forgiveness, and it's all in the past' card. She also said she'd done a lot of good stuff in the meantime and that was the reason she did all that stuff, to make amends. [She] knew at that point that I had started to go back to church," Leonard said. "I actually really thought that she would cooperate."

Leonard also told his brother, but "this time I didn't ask him. This time, I informed him I was doing something." Leonard's brother was upset, but Leonard didn't renege. In the meantime, their father had set up a meeting with other family members intending to confront their mother. He planned to do so under the guise of trying to get her some help for her alcohol use. Her parents were there, along with Leonard's uncle and his dad's sponsor. His father confronted her with the letter that Leonard had written to him. When Leonard explained to her again that he intended to have her registered as a sex offender, she went into the kitchen and grabbed a knife, then ran out of the house into the nearby forest and killed herself.

Leonard then felt compelled to tell his grandmother what had happened to his mother. He felt she deserved an explanation as to why there were so many police officers and a helicopter looking for his mother. Just as he had suspected in his youth, his grandmother struggled significantly to even comprehend what he was saying. She simply could not accept that a mother could do those types of things to her own child.

"It didn't compute for her. It took a couple of times of sitting down with her to explain it to her, retelling her what happened," Leonard said. "She didn't understand. She [was] like, 'But she was your mother?' 'Yes.' 'But she did this. But that doesn't make sense.' She really didn't understand. It took several people to explain it to her. My grandmother just didn't want to believe that these things even exist."

Today, Leonard is a middle-class professional who lives in the suburbs. Although he initially did not want children because of what he had heard about victims becoming offenders, he does have two healthy children and is happily married. Leonard reported that since talking more openly about his abuse, more and more of his memories are returning to him. "It's been hard, but at the same time my PTSD symptoms and [sleep] have been much better." He remains in treatment and still struggles with symptoms of complex PTSD, but believes he is getting healthier. He does admit that Mother's Day is still a bad day for him. "I'm always kind of pissy on Mother's Day."

Leonard is now back in touch with his faith and also with the teacher whom he first told about his mother's affair. In fact, she initiated the contact when she wrote him a letter of apology. "As it turned out, I mentioned her in my police report, and her boyfriend was the chief of the police at the time. I guess he mentioned my name or something. It was neat. She knows everything now."

To this day, Leonard's brother still refuses to talk about what happened.

Michael: "We Don't Talk About That Kind of Stuff"

Michael, 50, was raised in a loving home by Christian parents after being adopted at birth. His father was the pastor of a very busy and prominent church, which had a thriving congregation. He was often away from home, preparing sermons, attending board meetings, and performing weddings and funerals. Michael's mother was a nurse who tended primarily to the needs of Michael's older sister, who was troubled after having lived in multiple foster homes prior to her adoption.

Michael explained that although his parents were both very loving, they had been raised not to talk about their feelings and raised Michael to be the same. They regularly sent him messages like, "Don't rock the boat," "Don't go into that territory," and "God will take care of it." As a result, Michael grew up feeling alone, unworthy, unsupported, and unprotected.

One evening when Michael was 13, he was sexually abused by an elder in his father's church. He never told his parents, partly because of the messages he'd received but also because he knew they already had enough on their plate with his older sister. He didn't want to add to their problems. He also didn't feel confident that he would be supported, so he simply decided not to think about it.

Michael was reasonably successful at not thinking about the abuse for the next 35 years. It wasn't all that hard, especially since he didn't think it had any significant impact on him. However, as an adult, Michael grew to become an angry workaholic, whose negative attitude and behaviors eventually took a devastating toll on his marriage. When his wife of 17 years left him, he was both confused and hurt.

"I thought I would spend the rest of my life with her," he said. "I loved that woman and I wanted to be with her for the rest of my life, and she didn't even want to work on our marriage. She just ran away."

Michael's wife's leaving launched him into a process of self-exploration as he tried to make sense of what had gone so wrong in his life. He knew there was something wrong, that there must be some sort of explanation for his anger, but he didn't know what. In addition to beginning to actually read his Bible, Michael also began to read all kinds of other books on manhood, relationships, and God. He read anything he felt might help.

One day, a friend invited him to join an eight-member men's study group.

"The very first night I went, they were talking about the wounds and scars in men's lives and the fact that men don't typically like to talk about them," he said. "We prefer isolation, we don't face stuff. We run, hide, deny, avoid, bury, and repress. This was the beginning of me starting to realize some of that stuff. It didn't so much pop into my mind, the issue of being sexually molested, but I began realizing that wow, I've got issues."

Later that same year, another friend, who had a logging permit, invited Michael to go camping with him in the mountains. He wanted Michael along in case he hurt himself and needed to be rescued. During their trip, Michael's friend disclosed that he had been sexually abused as a boy and that he had struggled with it for more than 30 years. Michael was deeply impacted by his friend's disclosure. He began to recall his own abuse and examine the impact that it may have had on his life.

"It just hit me, and I knew God put me out there in the wilderness with this man for him to reveal to me something that I needed to look at. He was the very first person I ever shared my abuse with. It was 35 years later. It was overwhelming, but it was the beginning of taking those big steps towards healing, facing it, going into that wound."

Within a week, Michael shared his abuse story with his therapist and, a few weeks later, with his parents. He came to understand the confusion he had felt over having had his first sexual experience and his first orgasm with a man. Looking back, Michael was able to recognize that within months of the abuse occurring, his personality changed dramatically. He went from being a mild-mannered, soft-spoken, and faith-filled teenager to an irritable, angry, rebellious young man with a sudden interest in drinking, smoking pot, and having sex.

At the time, Michael simply attributed the changes he saw in himself to becoming a teenager. Although he never questioned whether he might be homosexual, after experiencing his first orgasm, he craved it and became sexually promiscuous with women. He also saw clearly how he'd tried to assert his heterosexuality through acting out with women, and how being sexually active became the platform by which he established an entire new set of friends. Michael recognized that he had numbed himself through the use of drugs and alcohol, and that not dealing with his abuse had likely cost him his marriage.

Michael explained that although his mother had questioned why his behavior had taken such a dramatic turn for the worse, her tone had seemed to imply that whatever was bothering him was likely his own fault. She never gave him the opportunity or permission to discuss what had happened nor the benefit of the doubt that it might not be his fault. "I wasn't given the feeling of 'hey, it's okay to be angry, but let's talk about why.'"

As a result, Michael remained silent. Silence seemed to work for him, at least for a while, since he only had a slight sense that anything was wrong anyway. He didn't understand that being abused was central to his character shift, and that his new rebellious behaviors were actually the coping mechanisms he used to suppress his pain.

"I was only abused one time, but it had a major impact on where I went in my life and how I handled life from that point on. Within months after being molested, I became very sexually promiscuous and started smoking pot and drinking. I didn't see that any of that was my way of avoiding my feelings. I was raised in a really good, strong Christian family. There wouldn't have been any other reason why I would have gone down that path."

Although Michael has not reconciled with his ex-wife, he is well on his way toward inner healing. He is a successful commercial real estate developer in the United States and has returned to his Christian roots. Yet, despite his progress, he still struggles to disclose his abuse to his closest friends. Many still have no idea he was ever abused.

"To talk about an experience like that with another man, with my close friends, would subject me to rejection, ridicule, abandonment, and jokes, things like that. I said something to my grandfather [my mother's dad] once, and he said, 'You shouldn't have told me that.' Two years ago, my biological father, who's been a part of my life for 15 years now, implied that I wanted it and that I enjoyed it and that it was something I asked for. It was very hurtful to get that from him."

Allen: "I Thought I was Going to be in Trouble"

Allen, 57, was eight years old when his father began using physical intimidation and death threats to force him to have sexual relations with his older sister, younger sister, and older brother while he watched. Allen explained that when things got to a certain point, his father would join in.

Like some of the others, Allen also initially didn't know that he was being sexually abused, and outside of what was happening at home, he lived an otherwise normal life. He developed friendships, played sports, and enjoyed many of the things that other teenage boys enjoy.

"I remember the first time I really realized how wrong it was. Friends at high school were talking about getting girlfriends and losing their virginity and stuff. My first experience was with my sister, and that's when I realized that's all f***ed up."

After hearing his friends talk about sex, Allen realized the nature of what was going on at home. He realized that what he was being forced to do with his two sisters and brother was abuse. Although he had been forced to engage in these acts, after learning they were inappropriate, Allen became consumed with shame, guilt, anger, and regret. He thought he was responsible, that he had sexually abused his younger sister. Allen didn't see himself as a victim; he saw himself as a perpetrator.

"I didn't see myself as the child, I saw myself as doing something wrong," he said. "I thought, I'm going to be in trouble. Even when it was happening, I knew it was wrong, but it was just kind of like a secret. I struggle to put it into words, to tell you the truth. I kind of contradict myself in the fact that I knew it was wrong, but it also just felt so normal."

Allen's mother had asked him if anything was going on, and he believes she knew, but he didn't say anything. He thought he was responsible.

"That's what got me, the age thing. Honestly, I think a lot of it was also the fear that my mom would be angry with me because I was the older one. By the time I realized my older sister had stopped, the (sexual)relationship with my younger sister was still going," he said. "I thought I was in trouble with the police, my school, everyone."

Prior to being abused, Allen had wrongfully been accused of committing a break-in. Their family had been away on holiday visiting friends when the friend's neighbor's house got broken into. The local police suspected it was Allen and brutally interrogated him. After that experience, Allen became very afraid of police, so going to them for help when he felt responsible for abusing his little sister was not an option. He assumed that he would be in trouble and that the police wouldn't believe him. Allen also worried that if his father were arrested, he would be responsible for breaking up the family. He was concerned that he and his siblings might be separated and put into foster care, where things could get worse.

Allen's extended family became aware of the situation after one of Allen's sisters, who was in high school, attempted suicide. She actually disclosed to their mother why she'd tried to kill herself, but their mother did nothing to intervene. A short while later at an extended family meeting, Allen overheard his aunts and uncles discussing his sister's suicide attempt and their sexual abuse. His uncle, who had a high-level position in the parliament, sent them home and none of them did anything either. Allen was shocked and saddened that nothing was done. When he and his siblings got home, their father beat them.

Soon after, Allen's mother and father got married. Allen had previously assumed they were already married. He believes his mother married his father to avoid having to testify if the matter ever went to court. (In many countries, including Canada, one spouse cannot be compelled to give evidence against the other.)

With nothing resolved, Allen struggled to make it through high school.

"When I left high school, I couldn't spell my middle name. That's because I played up so much at school, because I wanted attention," he said. "I was quiet at home because I was so afraid, especially [on] Sunday nights because that was when dad was drunk. But at school, I was the class clown."

After high school, Allen married, became a corrections officer, and had children of his own. "I've always tried to [do] the opposite of my father because I felt guilt. My father had been in prison, so I become a prison officer. My father never had anything to do with our schooling so I always went to my kid's school every Friday," Allen said. "I've tried to be so different from him, and I know it's guilt and shame 'cause I'm not like him."

Allen disclosed his abuse to his wife when he was 25 years old because he was committed to her and wanted her to know the "real" him. He didn't tell anyone else until he was 35, after his mother died. After her death, Allen began to struggle with aggression, and his wife asked him to go for counseling. He went but only for her sake.

"I did it only to shut the wife up," he said. "I didn't want to talk to anybody, but it was the best thing I ever did."

Allen found therapy to be very helpful. He had previously felt guilt and anxiety whenever he had to change his daughter's diapers. Therapy helped him to understand he was simply tending to his infant daughter's needs, not doing anything wrong.

Although his marriage ended during his healing process, Allen's ex-wife is supportive of his recovery process. Allen now facilitates support groups for sexually abused men in the prison where he works. He is well respected in the male survivor community and is very close with his older sister. He still struggles with feelings of guilt associated with relating to his younger sister and does not have a relationship with her.

About six years prior to our interview, Allen did a favor for his older sister. At her request, Allen went to their father's house to get something. Allen was shocked at his father's response to him. "I pulled in his drive, I was standing at my driver's door, and he came up to me and he said, 'I know you kids have forgiven me, and I'm going to leave [your sister] an extra something in my will as an apology, but I know she wanted it.'" Allen was filled with disgust at his father's belief that she had welcomed the abuse. He hasn't told his sister.

Julien: "He Stole My Voice"

Julien, a French Canadian in his mid-forties, described himself as a naïve and trusting person who grew up in a loving, middle-class home. His parents held Christian values and had strong ties to the Catholic Church. Although his parents were very loving toward all of their children, as the third of six children, Julien sometimes felt he lacked for attention.

Julien's mother worked for their priest, who was also a trusted friend that visited their family home on a weekly basis. The priest noticed Julien's desire for more attention and offered to spend extra time with him. When Julien was 16, their priest began taking him out for meals. He also taught him to downhill ski, took him to the pool, away on weekend ski trips, and eventually to his private cabin. Their relationship developed without incident for the first year, until the priest invited Julien into his bedroom. He pretended he needed a book, then locked the door, turned on some music, and began to wrestle and play fight with Julien. He then started to press against Julien's pants and genitals. Julien was shocked.

"I froze, you know, I froze like an animal. I recall my body being rigid, I couldn't move," Julien said. "I could only hear my heartbeat, and my breathing was hard, and I had his hands moving all over my body, and he ejaculated."

The priest then fondled Julien as he masturbated himself. Afterwards, the priest began to cry, and discussed how he couldn't perform mass anymore, and went on to discuss how Julien had "asked for it." Coming from their priest, "those words are very powerful," Julien said. They stayed with him for many years.

On their drive home, the priest also spoke about how he was now doomed because of the sin he had just committed. He told Julien not to discuss it with anyone, and Julien complied. A short while later that same day, he called and asked to speak to Julien. He told Julien that he had phoned his superior and received absolution over the phone after confessing his sin. Julien felt manipulated by his priest's abuse and his instant plea for forgiveness.

A few weeks later, Julien saw the priest with a much younger boy in his car. This was all the proof Julien needed to show him that the abuse had been planned. Julien wondered how many other young boys had been abused by him but remained silent.

"What the priest did was take my voice away and steal my innocence. Nobody knew that I was sexually abused. I couldn't talk about it."

Unaware of what had taken place, Julien's mother continued to work with their priest and continued to invite him into their home. Julien simply stayed away from him. Only his older sister noticed, "She could read me like a book. She took me aside and asked me about it."

Julien didn't recall whether he made up a story or told her, but he did recall that he made her promise not to tell their parents, and she kept that promise.

In college, Julien finally sought help. He was very distracted by what had happened to him and was struggling to cope. Unfortunately, the abuse he experienced at the hands of his priest also opened the door for other abusers to take advantage of him. When Julien went for therapy, his counselor invited him to "reenact" what had happened to him, and Julien, who believed his therapist was attempting to help him, was abused for a second time.

"It was an older man. When I told him about the abuse, his way to heal, his technique, was to reenact. So here I am talking about my abuse, and he's half naked. We're sitting on the ground, redoing what the abuser did. Then he gave a hug, and he had an erection himself."

This abuse likely would have continued had the counselor not left his practice before Julien's next session. Julien's new therapist correctly informed him of the unethical and abusive nature of his previous therapist. Julien became further discouraged and threw himself into his studies.

SECONDARY TRAUMA/INJURY

When someone who is already feeling vulnerable discloses abuse and is met with further abuse or a dismissive, disbelieving, unsupportive, or hostile response, it causes an emotional injury.[103] Secondary injuries can impact victims in worse ways than their initial abuse.

Being abused by someone you turn to for help, being told you are lying, or being dismissed can lead to long-term mental health issues. It can also deter victims from making further attempts to disclose.[104, 105]

"At that point, it was like a garbage can," he said. "I put the lid on it and put it aside. I focused on the university. Keeping busy was good. I didn't want to feel," he said. "I didn't do any therapy for a while, but I did have other [sexual] experiences with men where I would say I was not in charge. [They would] just initiate eye contact or touch, and I [would] follow them and they [would have their way]. Then I [would] feel dirty and shameful and [guilty]."

Before graduating, Julien was sexually assaulted again by an uncle who was visiting for New Year's Eve. Because they had such a large family, people would often split up to sleep in different places. This particular uncle offered to take the twin bed in Julien's room while his wife and baby slept in the living room with Julien's sister.

"It was New Year's Eve, so people were drunk. I was sleeping, but he got his hand moving and explored through my underwear. It was hard to fake sleeping. My heart, it was beating so loud. I wanted it to stop beating. I couldn't say anything. Then he took my hand and he put it on his erect penis, and he came."

Once again, Julien felt powerless to stop it. After getting what he wanted the first time, Julien's uncle continued to abuse him like this on subsequent visits.

When Julien was 30, he finally confronted his uncle, and the abuse stopped. "It was good," Julien said. "He left me alone after that."

Despite the fact that he ended it, Julien felt tremendous shame that he had "let" the abuse continue for so long. He saw himself as weak because he hadn't been able to refuse his uncle's advances, and he worried what others would think of him if they knew.

In the 1990s, Julien decided to pursue charges against the priest, who was now in charge of a youth and family center and a parish. "The whole trial was hush-hush. Lawyers meeting lawyers at the airport hotel. It was not even in front of the bishop," Julien said. The person they assigned to defend Julien was his offender's best friend, another priest. "They ended up getting a psychologist, a very high-[ranking] one to write a report about me, even though he'd never met me. The psychologist tried to play with my age. It was revictimizing."

Several years later, Julien worked with another therapist, who again invalidated his reality.

"This therapist knew nothing about sexual abuse. I spent two years of my time educating him, then he ended up telling me I was 'not authentic.'"

When Julien married, he knew he didn't want to keep secrets from his wife, so he told her about his abuse. She didn't understand and questioned him, saying, "You were that age? Why couldn't you just say no?"

When Julien became a parent himself, he became consumed with a new kind of fear. "When I had my first son, it triggered me, the birth of a child. Holy sh*t, I'm gonna have to protect him. Everybody was saying my son was beautiful. I didn't want him to be beautiful. I didn't want him to be attractive to a pedophile."

To this day, Julien struggles with self-blame for "letting" the abuse occur in the first place and for letting it go on so long. Although he married and had children, he eventually came to accept that he is more attracted to men. He ended his marriage and is now in a same-sex relationship.

PART 3

BARRIERS TO DISCLOSURE

WHY MEN DON'T DISCUSS SEXUAL ABUSE

Although their responses to being abused varied, each of the men I spoke to reported deep-rooted, complex barriers to disclosure, which existed across multiple domains over their entire lifetime. When I asked each to explain the reasons they hadn't disclosed their abuse sooner, the most common reason was that they had either been too physiologically traumatized and/or they had experienced intense feelings of fear.

A fear/trauma response was conveyed by each, but in two distinct ways, depending on whether or not they had blocked the memories of their abuse. Those who experienced memory loss or extreme dissociation experienced this (the memory loss/dissociation) as an extreme physiological response to the traumas which were simply too much to endure. They blocked their memories and developed illnesses like dissociative identity disorder or a conversion disorder.

The men who had remained aware of their abuse, even if they didn't understand it, also experienced significant physical, physiological, and emotional symptoms of distress. Within their fear and trauma response, these two categories of men most often reported, in order of prevalence, the following reasons for their silence: (a) loss of memory, (b) fear of being blamed, (c) the abuse was too difficult to discuss, (d) an attempt at disclosure had ended badly, (e) fear of worse consequences, (f) fear of not being believed, and (g) fear of their perpetrator. They also cited shame, a desire to protect their family, and a lack of understanding about abuse, among the other significant reasons for their nondisclosure.

I Didn't Remember

More than half of the men reported involuntary memory loss in regard to all or some of the abuse they had experienced. Each of these men had little or no recollection of certain periods in their lives when the abuse happened, though all had recovered some memories. Three participants developed dissociative identity disorder, which helped them manage their traumatic experiences. A fourth developed a conversion disorder, which disappeared shortly after his memories returned. One participant reported having only "flashes" or "glimpses" of his initial abuse, while another reported having no memory of his childhood. Two other men reported purposefully trying to forget the abuse; although they were successful for a period of time, their memories ultimately resurfaced.

I Thought I Would Be Blamed

Eight of the men I spoke to stated they hadn't disclosed their abuse to any-one, in part because they felt responsible for their level of "participation", or for not having stopped it sooner.

Ricky was one of these men. He worried he would be in trouble with his father for not ending it sooner. Although he had been traumatized the first several times his cousin abused him, he'd experienced the pleasurable sensation of ejaculation and enjoyed the nonsexual attention he got from his cousin. He eventually stopped trying to fight his cousin off. Ricky's father was extremely homophobic and likely would not have understood.

Jacob also feared his father might blame and beat him. Also, "I thought it was my fault. I remember saying, 'What am I going to do if dad finds out?' I felt guilty. Absolutely, I thought it was totally my fault. I had f***ed my mother. How could I do that?"

Allen, who had been forced by his father to engage in sexual acts with his siblings felt responsible for abusing his younger sister. He worried he'd be in trouble with the police. Aaron too, he didn't want to get in trouble for participating in sexual acts and for talking about sexual matters.

It Was Too Difficult to Discuss

Michael, who was abused by a man in his father's church, initially didn't understand the impact his abuse had on him. Still, he didn't want to have to revisit the situation. "I chose to continue to run because it seemed like the path of least resistance, and the one that would be least painful."

Anthony had similar thoughts. His sister was five years old when their father stopped abusing her and started abusing him. When they were both adults she came to him and asked if he'd been abused. When he confirmed that he had, she apologized for not having protected him from their father and soon after committed suicide. Having already attempted suicide at such a young age himself, he felt like his abuse was something he should not talk about. "It seemed to me that talking about being sexually abused was dangerous," he said. "Talk about it and it will kill you."

Ricky also hadn't wanted to discuss his abuse with his parents when it first occurred. "I just didn't want to deal with it myself. I put it out of my head," he said. "It just never happened."

Even as an adult in therapy, Jacob still doesn't want to talk about his mom. "I didn't want to go back and live that all over again."

An Attempt at Disclosure Had Ended Badly

Despite being fearful, some men tested potential confidants by first disclosing lesser pieces of information. Most of the hopefuls didn't pass the test. Leonard told his teacher about his mother's affair and the teacher called his mother—who then beat him. Leonard's teacher failed his test of trust.

A week after he was abused by his coach, Aaron went to his school guidance counselor to warn him not to send other youth to the same camp. The counselor, in response, absolved Aaron of his "sins" and told him not to discuss it with anyone else. Aaron was made to feel responsible. He later learned the counselor was also molesting children and likely covering for the coach, his fellow offender.

Jacob, who was abused by his mother, was abducted by a stranger while on his way to school. He relayed the information to his vice principal, but nothing was done to help. Several others also failed to intervene on separate occasions.

When Josh disclosed his abuse, his therapist, a clinical psychologist, dismissed his abuse as "the way children play together." Josh told the therapist, "I think I was abused" and then explained why. "I told him what happened with my cousin. His response was 'All cousins do sex play.' Done! Boom! That was it."

These boys and men based their decision about whether or not to disclose further information on how well their potential confidant responded. None of them received a good response, and each remained silent for years to come.

I Knew Things Could Get Worse

Over half of the men worried that things might end up worse for them if they were to tell anyone about their abuse. Some feared that the punishment they would receive, if they failed to escape their abuser, would make things worse for them, especially if the offender was their parent. Others feared what would happen if they were to break up the family.

Jacob believed that no one would ever be able to rescue him. He said resources were not in place to support him. In those days children did not get removed from their parents' care.

Leonard worried he might be separated from his siblings and placed in a foster home, where he knew he and his siblings might face worse abuse.

Garrett had similar fears, and he wanted a better life for himself. He relied on his parents' financial support to fund college and made the decision to remain silent to ensure he kept it. "Part of me thought that my whole world would collapse," he said.

When Josh was abused for a third time as an adult in Africa, he didn't say anything because he feared the very real threat of being arrested or killed. He did not report the abuse to the Peace Corps because he feared he'd lose his emergency support and not be welcome back.

No One Will Believe Me

In their earlier years, six men were convinced they would not be believed if they revealed their abuse. This was especially true if the people who abused them were the very people they were supposed to be able to trust—the people who were supposed to be protecting them from harm. These betrayals of trust impacted their ability to trust others.

In his adolescent years, Garrett was teased by his peers for being "creepy and socially awkward. It didn't create a sense that it was safe to be vulnerable around people. I didn't trust anyone based on getting rejected left and right by my peers." His teachers, who otherwise could have been sources of help, told him that he was "odd." He also knew that his parents were very good at manipulating authority figures. "They knew all my coaches and supposedly had good relationships with these coaches who maybe I could have opened up to." No one gave him the sense that he could turn to them for support.

Ricky saw what happened when other people disclosed abuse: They were met with disbelief and distrust. "I hate to use the word 'victim,' but the victim usually becomes the bad guy," he said. "It was painful enough what I was going through inside. I didn't want to add to it."

Aaron worried that the age and power difference between him and his abuser might influence his parents' willingness to believe him. "I was feeling like, you know, they wouldn't believe me," he said. "He was this 'man's man' who they respected, and I was just a kid."

Although Jacob was involved with an agency that supports male victims of sexual abuse and was being asked to discuss his experience of abuse, he still feared he might be thought of as embellishing the truth. When he shared he began by saying, "I know it sounds hard to believe." He also worried that if people did believe him, they would think he was crazy or perverted. In his youth, because of his negative experiences with people in positions to help, Jacob actually reminded himself not to trust anyone.

"I mean, I actually said to myself, don't trust anyone. Ever!"

I Was Scared of My Perpetrator(s)

Six of the men were victimized by their biological parents—three by their fathers and three by their mothers. Not unlike those who had nonfamilial offenders, these men reported that as boys, their parent (either the offender or their non-sexually offending parent) had used violence or the threat of violence to control them. For a few, violence, threats, and abuse occurred on a daily basis, and the fear they felt was profound.

Jacob knew from a very early age that he had to cooperate with his mother's abuse if he wanted to be fed and didn't want to be beaten.

Phillip too, he witnessed the way his father "went off" on others in public. "I used to just cringe. I'd be in a public place and he'd take somebody on, and I'd just want to crawl in a hole and hide. I was always afraid when I came home. I was always waiting to be slammed around for something whether I'd done it or not."

Garrett's father wasn't sexually abusing him but was still very scary. His father threatened to kill Garrett if he didn't attend to his mother's every need.

Even though Allen grew to be 6'3" as an adult and towered over his father, who was now elderly, he still feared him. "It's just that power he still has over you," Allen said. "About two years ago I saw him walking down the main street, and I was still afraid of him. I'm twice his size. He was 80 years old and I was still afraid of him."

I Felt Too Ashamed

Victims of sexual abuse have a two-fold experience of shame: They experience shame about having been abused and shame at the thought of disclosing their abuse. The shame of victimhood was described by these men as 'paralyzing' and an emotion 'as powerful as fear.'

All of the men reported experiencing shame (often associated with an over-estimation of their level of responsibility) at some point in their lives. The feeling was especially strong if they also questioned their level of partic-ipation in the abuse, if they felt aroused or ejaculated during the abuse, or if they thought they should or could have stopped it sooner.

The strong emotions and physiological sensations these men experienced as boys paralyzed them. As boys, they had been coerced into sexual situations with lies, physical force and threats to their safety, or to the safety of those they loved. As a result, they experienced shame, guilt, confusion and poor self-image and were concerned about how others would perceive them if they told the truth.

Despite the fact Jacob had been seeing a therapist for two years, he didn't speak to her about his experiences of abuse because he was too ashamed. He still thought it was his fault.

Julien felt the same way. "It was too big, too much shame," he said. "Shame and guilt. It's like the darkness of the cloud is so big that you don't see the light. You can't see the light."

Leonard initially believed that exposing his abuse would leave him com-pletely vulnerable and unprotected. "I didn't want to tell anybody because I didn't want their pity. Worst of all, there's a particular look in their eyes that I never wanted to deal with. I mean, it happened, I was angry about it but pity just made it worse."

Gordon relayed similar sentiments. "You didn't talk about it. I mean it's just something you don't talk about. It's your dirty little secret. I think it's the shame factor, that I'm something bad because that happened to me."

Those who experienced shame also perceived themselves in a painfully diminished manner, which was exacerbated by their sense of responsibility. Words of accusation, blame or even kindness spoken to them as they were being victimized, often led them to feel confused and responsible. The result of this was that their self-perceptions became distorted. Several reported feeling lesser, not because they believed something bad had *happened* to them, but because they believed they *were* bad.[106]

SHAME

Researcher, and author Brené Brown identifies shame as the feeling "I am bad" or "I am somehow not good enough." She explains that shame is "a fear of disconnection," whereas guilt is "I did something wrong." Shame triggers a fear of rejection and is felt from the inside out. Victims even experience shame when no one is watching.[107] Shame is one of the most powerful and disturbing human emotions, the experience of which involves seeing oneself as both painfully diminished and overly transparent to others.[108] Because it is so distressing, people often try to hide it from view, escape, or even deny that it exists. Shame often feels impossible to discuss since it is self-validating.[109] In the moment that people feel shame, they also feel they deserve to feel badly.[110] Victims of childhood sexual abuse re-experience the shame that they so desperately long to escape. Such was the case for the men in this research.

Michael described his abuse as "embarrassing" and a very personal issue that he did not want his friends to know about. He still feels this way even to this day. Anthony reported feeling shame because his abuse "seemed homosexual." Aaron feared going to his high school prom, that it was "branded on my forehead" and that everyone "would know that it happened to me." Ricky stated, "You know, there's someone fondling me and touching me, I'm like embarrassed 'cause I'm naked and my penis is in somebody's mouth, you know, it's a little embarrassing."

Josh explained, "I just remember being humiliated and feeling embarrassed about ever telling anybody. Even today it's kind of hard for me to tell someone, especially a woman, because I feel like it makes me seem like a total creep."

Feelings of shame, guilt and confusion were especially prominent among those whose parents had taught them not to talk about sex. As boys, they oscillated between wondering if they had been victimized and wondering if they had done something wrong.

DAMAGED GOODS

Men in this research supported what Brené Brown said about victims feeling lesser or inferior.[iii] They too felt devalued by their offenders who isolated and then used them for their own sexual gratification. Because these men felt devalued by their offenders, they worried that others would view them this same way.

Although childhood sexual abuse impacts boys and men in ways that are similar to how it impacts girls and women, there are also some distinct differences. For example, males are commonly bothered by the myth that boys who are sexually abused grow up to become offenders themselves. Conversely, society does not generally fear that sexually abused women will grow up to become rapists or pedophiles.

I Didn't Want to Be Judged

Unlike female sexual abuse victims, male sexual abuse victims are often silenced by the myth that boys who are sexually abused will grow up to sexually abuse others. Some of the men I interviewed feared being viewed as future predators. Others remained silent in part to avoid being stigmatized. Phillip stated, "I didn't want people to know that had happened to me. There's a stigma, or there was. It's becoming less, but there's a stigma about having been abused."

Ricky explained that he didn't want people looking at him differently. "People sometimes want to know gory details. I didn't want to be judged. Nobody wants to be judged. I hate to use the analogy of rape, but people always judge the rape victim."

Leonard worried he would be thought of as a future pedophile. "By the time I was 15, I really liked to read, and there was a fair bit of literature at the time about abusers having been abused, so the automatic assumption is always drawn— 'Oh, you were abused, you are going to be a pedophile'— and I would not deal well with that." Leonard also believed that exposing his abuse would have left him completely vulnerable and unprotected. He remained silent in part because no one knew what was happening to him at home. He pretended that everything was normal and maintained the illusion that he was alright. Sustaining this illusion helped him to survive.

VICTIM-OFFENDERS

Despite the fact that many offenders report having been abused themselves, the idea that men who were abused as youth are destined to become offenders is not supported by research. Only a small percentage (approx. 9%) of victims go on to offend.[112] Although none of the men in this study worried they would become offenders, one worried others might think he would.

When Aaron was starting his career as a lawyer, he feared the personal and professional consequences of disclosing his abuse. "I didn't want anybody to know, especially not professionally. I was so afraid. Can you imagine if that came out in the middle of a trial? I was in the frigging courthouse prosecuting child sex crimes cases, and I was afraid that somebody was going to walk in, tell somebody, and somehow my name was going to be on a document and it would be everywhere. It would destroy my career."

In the end one of Aaron's worst fears came true. He was judged for having been victimized. Despite the fact that he completed all the relevant training, he was denied the opportunity to become an expert witness in his unit. His superior feared he would not be able to be impartial toward sex offenders since he'd been a victim himself. Aaron felt betrayed. He had studied sex offenders and come to understand them as sick people in need of help. "It was like somebody sticking a gun in your face, robbing you of your stuff and people blaming you because you weren't wearing a bulletproof vest or something."

I Felt Responsible

Feeling responsible for something involves having a perceived sense of control over other people or a situation. It often includes a sense of shame and guilt.

Josh felt both of those emotions for having taken risks while traveling, and for placing himself in a vulnerable situation. He was traveling in a country where homosexuality is a crime, and had openly identified as gay/bisexual. Plus, he had trusted a complete stranger enough to get high with him. "It's my own d*mn fault," he recalled thinking.

Allen's shame coexisted with the knowledge that his first intimate experience was with his sister. He worried that his friends would abandon him if they knew.

This was similar for Leon. "The shame is, I think, as you develop and mature, you feel like you did something wrong. Like you did something that contributed to this. You feel tremendous guilt and tremendous shame."

Based on the teasing and rejection Garrett experienced, he too, initially felt responsible. "I guess on some level I blamed myself for what was going on and felt ashamed and guilty. I thought that it must be about me, so if I told anyone that, that would be further evidence of how screwed up I am."

As a Catholic, Anthony felt the weight of the fact that he couldn't forgive his abuser. "I didn't want to feel like I was a bad Catholic. That was important to me. So, at 38 I went to the priest and confessed. The priest was the first person I ever told [intentionally] about having been sexually abused by my father. The priest said, 'It is not a sin not to forgive him for this. It's fine for you not to forgive him.'"

I Was Confused

Although some of the men did not discuss it explicitly, each of those who had experienced arousal during the abuse relayed feelings of guilt, confusion, or fear at the thought of getting in trouble. The trust and fondness each of these men had felt toward their abuser prior to the abuse, coupled with the physiological arousal they felt during the abuse, left them with complex, mixed and unresolved emotions.

Aaron, who was assaulted by a coach whom he had previously trusted and admired, said he had a profound sense of shame, guilt and failure for not predicting and preventing the abuse. He blamed himself "for not being smart enough or man enough to stop it, and for (his) body betraying (him). Like, why was I aroused? How come I came? Why did that happen? What's wrong with me?"

Aaron's abuser was particularly manipulative. He appealed to Aaron's idea of what it meant to be a man, gave Aaron pornographic magazines and alcohol, then implied Aaron should masturbate. Aaron was doing just that when the coach walked in. "It totally shocked me. I started shaking, and he's like, 'What are you so nervous about? This is normal.'" In a manly voice, the coach stated, "I mean, it's what guys do, don't worry about it."

"He sat down next to me and started going through the pictures with me. He started showing me more and more graphic magazines: men on men, women on women, and all sorts of stuff. I was like, 'What is all of this?' And he goes, 'It's just sex, don't worry about it. Just be a man. Why are you such a wimp?' You know, that kind of stuff. Then he touched me and performed oral sex on me. I felt like my body was betraying me and I just wanted to disappear. I literally tried to curl up in a ball and cover my head with the blankets and pillows. You know, just feeling like there was no escape. I'm in the middle of nowhere. He's my ride home. I mean, there's no phones, no cell phones, nothing," Aaron said.

"He had this leering disgusting look in his eye, this lascivious look in his eye. I mean, it always bothered me. It was like it was haunting me, so I just shut down sexually. I stayed away from everybody. I thought that's what made somebody gay. I didn't know anything about sexuality at the time."

Prior to being abused, he had a girlfriend and was fully heterosexual. After, he questioned his sexual identity and now identifies as bisexual.

Michael, whose abuser attended his father's church, was similarly confused about his arousal. "It was not only painful, but it was extremely confusing because it was the first time I'd ever had an orgasm—the first time I'd ever had those feelings of arousal and excitement and the pleasure," he said. "It was confusing because it was from another man. I didn't get it. I didn't know what to do about that. I just remember that feeling, that sexual pleasure, the release from orgasm, and I just kind of craved that."

These men didn't initially understand that men could experience physiological arousal while being traumatized, and they feared others wouldn't understand it either.

Discussions About Sex Were Off Limits

Six men said that a major reason they didn't disclose their abuse sooner was because sex was a forbidden topic in their home. Gordon said discussions about sex are still forbidden in his small Southern Baptist community. "We're not allowed to talk about anything," he said. "Sex is still a taboo topic, even in sexual education classes. You can't even talk about things like condom usage and things like that...just abstinence."

Phillip said he grew up in "different times" when no one discussed sexual abuse. "No one talked about sexual abuse in the 1940s, let alone male abuse. Even if they would have, there were no resources for male sexual abuse victims. Society simply did not recognize that men could be victims too."

I Enjoyed Nonsexual Aspects of the Relationship

Some of the men enjoyed certain nonsexual aspects of their abusive relationships, particularly if they lacked attention or affection as boys. As Ricky explained, "I mean here's somebody that I admire, that I love, you know, cared about, showing me some affection. Here's somebody paying attention to me, showing me some consideration. It felt good emotionally for somebody to take an interest in me. I didn't realize that he was using me."

Anthony said the fellow patient who abused him in treatment gave him a level of attention that he wasn't used to, and that he liked, so he didn't push him away. "The sexual things I didn't like, but he also held me and he sang to me, and I did like that."

Leon had a similar experience. His abusers also filled an emotional need. "There was an affection I had for both of these men as a child. I think there was sort of a feeling of pleasing them and giving them gratification. You know, if I take care of you, you'll take care of me, or I'll get more gifts, or I'll get more admiration and support. I think that certainly was part of the dynamic."

INITIATING REVICTIMIZATION

Many abuse survivors "initiate" their own revictimization by seeking out their offenders. They do so not for sexual gratification but because their offenders meet their need for affection. Others comply with their abusers to avoid losing the relationship or facing other consequences like homelessness.[113] Three men reported they felt compelled to comply with their offender because they relied on them for emotional support and attention.

The guilt these men felt over having enjoyed the relationship contributed to confusion about their sexuality.

I Felt Alone

Several of these men had little or no hope as boys that anyone would ever help them: (a) They believed there was no point and no one would help, (b) their non-sexually abusive parent was emotionally unavailable, and/or (c) they felt trapped because their abuser kept them isolated and dependent.

A few of the men recalled circumstances in their youth when adults had the chance to see that something wasn't right, yet did nothing to help. When these adults, some of whom were authority figures, failed to rescue them, it deepened their sense of hopelessness and isolation. Others felt isolated and hopeless because they believed there was something wrong with them or because they didn't have the social skills to relate to their peers.

Garrett knew he was missing out on normal social relationships. "I felt like I was on Mars," he said. "I was a very good student, great athlete, but for whatever reason I just couldn't relate to people in a functional way. My attempts at friendships were pretty much rejected so I kind of retreated." Garrett wondered, "Am I invisible? Isn't there anyone in the world that can see that I'm not okay?"

Anthony had a similar experience, "I just couldn't relate to other children. I couldn't really relate to anybody. I didn't have friends. I was a very isolated, lonely kid."

When Aaron returned to school after experiencing abuse at summer camp his ability to maintain a social life changed. He too, felt isolated from his peers and began to think that something was wrong with him. His abuse made the already complicated feelings of being a teenager even more complex. "It was like a force multiplier of all the things you normally go through in puberty and teenage years, but it just made it so much worse," he said. "I thought I was the only one this ever happened to, like I am so bad, so damaged, so worthless."

Julien said his abuser "stole my innocence, my trust, my childhood. He robbed me from the friendships that teenagers have. I felt I had to keep the secret. I was the dirty one. It's huge."

Although Leon appeared social, he said it was a façade, that deep down he felt very lonely and isolated. Several others had similar experiences. They stated that although they had social lives, they felt like they were alone in the world, like they were the only ones this had ever happened to.

The isolation and hopelessness these men felt as boys was profound. Several explained they simply grew up accustomed to not having anyone be there for them, including their own families.

Ricky's feelings of isolation were in part because he knew he couldn't talk to his parents about his abuse. He reasoned that if he couldn't tell his own parents, who could he tell? Leonard felt similarly. "I wouldn't have known who to tell," he said. "I mean, this is going on at home. Where else are you supposed to go?" Phillip stated that it never even occurred to him that he could tell anyone.

It Felt Like There Was No Point in Telling

The belief that no one would help, especially if their abuser was a parent or they already had bad experiences reaching out, was the second most common reason for these men not telling anyone about their abuse.

Jacob's grandmother walked in on him being anally raped by their priest but did nothing. His principal failed him at least twice when he reached out for help. By the time the surgeon and psychiatrist tried to intervene, Jacob had no faith they would be successful and refused to cooperate. Allen's family turned a blind eye and sent him and his siblings home with their abusers. His mother then married his abusive father, which Allen believes she did so she couldn't be compelled to testify about the abuse.

My Non-sexually Abusive Parent Was Emotionally Unavailable

Seven of the 13 men reported having at least one non-sexually abusive parent to live with. Of these, the majority described their non-sexually abusive parents as either emotionally unavailable to them, physically abusive toward them, or both.

Anthony, who was sexually abused by his father from infancy, was neglected and physically and emotionally abused by his mother. "My mother was a drug addict. She was on prescription drugs most of my life. She was very, very erratic. I knew to keep away from her. I don't really know what she understood. She was very ill. She would stay in bed for days staring at the ceiling. I knew that was a time not to bother her. Before I learned that, that could get me smacked around quite a bit, but after I figured that out I just left her alone."

Although Michael wasn't abused by either of his parents, he described both as being emotionally unavailable to him. "I felt a feeling of abandonment," he said. "I mean, I was as close to them as anybody else, but yet there wasn't a feeling of safety or an ability to really talk about deep and meaningful feelings and emotions."

Ricky's mother was seriously ill. He grew up with the understanding that not only was his mother not available to him, but also that he had to stay out of his father's way as he tended to her. "The cycle is supposed to be you're cared for by your parents, you care for yourself, and then you care for your parents," he said. "I cared for my parents through my whole childhood and most of my adult life. I've been the parent since I was a child."

Phillip did not remember ever coming home to parents that were happy to see him. "I wasn't being nurtured and taken care of by them," he said. "I was being used as an instrument for them."

I Felt Trapped

Seven men said they never spoke up because they didn't want to disrupt the family system on which they were dependent. Two said their parent-abuser kept them isolated and dependent. Jacob knew he had to cooperate with his mother-abuser if he wanted to eat.

Garrett's dependence extended into his adulthood; he knew very little about how to take care of himself, and needed his parents to pay for his university education if he was ever to be independent.

"I wasn't prepared to be on my own. I never really had many of the building block experiences to not depend on them," he said. "Growing up, I was brainwashed to think that any help or contact outside the nuclear family was just very dangerous. Not only dangerous, it would never help me."

I Didn't Understand It

More than half of the men interviewed grew up unaware of either (a) the impact of their abuse or (b) the fact that their abuse was sexual in nature. Several provided examples of the profound effect their abuse had on their lives, but said they did not understand it until much later in life even though they had experienced significant symptoms in the aftermath.

Michael was in his forties when he finally came to see that his abuse experience changed his entire personality. "Initially, it didn't seem like it was worth talking about. I didn't see a connection," he said. "I honestly didn't think that being molested that one night would, or could, possibly result in what has come to be reality [and at the root] of many of the things that had happened in my life." Leon initially had no idea that he was being abused, nor that his abuse was the reason that he drank daily for the next three and a half decades.

While most recognized that they were being physically abused, a few had no idea that what they were experiencing was sexual until much later. Two of the men, whose abuse began very early in life, went on to lead very isolated lives. Neither had close friends with whom to compare notes, and each assumed that what they were experiencing at home was normal.

Leonard said, "If it was something out of the ordinary, like I've got other uncles, so if one particular uncle had abused me and the others didn't, I would have realized it was out of the ordinary. Not having another mother, I had no comparison, so I just assumed that well, everyone else does this too. I didn't understand at the time that anything wrong was happening. I didn't like it, but I didn't like eating vegetables either."

Anthony learned about the sexual nature of his abuse from his therapist. "Up until the age of 53 I had pornographic photographs of myself that my father had taken. I never realized they were pornographic. I had some inkling that they were important so I showed them to my therapist at the time, who confirmed what they were pictures of, and then I ripped them up, but I had had them for years."

Although Garrett grew up knowing that he was being abused, he was 27 before he recognized the sexual nature of his abuse. "I mean, I knew enough to know that something was very, very wrong. I just didn't know how to describe it."

I Wanted to Protect My Family

Of the men who understood they were being sexually abused, each didn't discuss their abuse either to (a) protect their family's reputation or their own sense of family, or to (b) protect their parents from information they thought would be too hard for them to handle. Nine of the men remembered keeping silent in part to maintain the illusion that their family was perfect, or because they didn't want to break up the family.

Michael worried about his family's reputation if he disclosed. "I didn't want to cause a stink," he said. "[My abuser] and my parents were friends. My dad's church was a thriving congregation. I just kind of let it be. I just felt like if I said something it would cause all kinds of commotion. I wouldn't be believed, and it would be an embarrassment to the family [and] to my father in his position as a pastor."

Julien also wanted to protect his family's reputation. The whole community knew his mother, who was a teacher, and he was expected to be a role model to other students. Even as an adult, he chose to keep the matter private to protect his family.

Gordon didn't want to cause any familial ruptures by saying something. "You can't un-ring that bell. Even though nobody's in that harmonious of a relationship, you just don't want to break up the family and have this part of the family be not speaking to you."

Allen feared that his father would be arrested and jailed and that his siblings would be separated and sent to foster care. He didn't want to upset his mother or be separated from his siblings. "Family's supposed to take care of each other," Allen said. "You're supposed to pretend everything's wonderful."

Three of the men abused by people outside of their immediate family recalled not wanting to burden their families with their problems. For Ricky, who lived with his grandmother, this feeling was particularly strong. His mother's health was poor and he felt like his father had enough on his plate. "My mother was always on the verge of dying," he said. "They had enough problems. They didn't need my problems."

Josh, whose father also had health issues, was actually deterred from burdening his family. He was aware that he was the unplanned, youngest child and was often reminded of the fact that he had created a burden. He grew up feeling like he didn't have the right to ask anything more of his family. He also knew his father wouldn't want to hear about the abuse.

"I knew on a visceral level, reactive, instinctively, that telling my father would hurt him and potentially kill him. I actually had a sense that I wasn't being melodramatic. At the time, he was already on heart attack number eight or nine. So as a family we'd been doing everything very gently. Tiptoeing around. I certainly didn't want to aggravate that."

Seven others also felt the need to protect their parent(s) from information they thought would be too hard for them to handle. Ricky worried about disappointing his father, who was very religious. "The idea of two guys having sex is utterly repugnant to him."

Gordon worried about his mother, who was a single parent at the time. "In all honesty, I would have never disclosed to her because I knew how bad it would have hurt her," he said.

Even as an adult, Leonard continued to protect his father, a longtime alcoholic who had finally gotten sober. "I just didn't want him to start drinking again. It was slowly killing him." Leonard said.

Julien also didn't want to risk causing pain to his family. When he finally did disclose the truth his worst fear came true. "I still recall my mom's reaction when I told her. She had to go to her bedroom and cry," he said. "It was very emotional because she was very close to that uncle. She said it was like I took a sledge hammer and hit her in the forehead."

An Overall Look at the Barriers Men Face

Overall, the men reported deep-rooted, complex barriers that existed across multiple domains over their entire lifetime. Although each of their responses to their abuse varied, each reported having significant emotional and physiological responses in its aftermath. Significantly, the most predominant barrier was that of either involuntary or voluntary memory loss associated with what they perceived to be unbearably traumatic events.

Apart from memory loss, several men explained that their abuse was simply too difficult to discuss. Some had tested the waters to see if they could trust someone to respond favorably, but their test ended badly. As boys, more than half of the men presumed they would not be believed. Others felt strongly that they could never disclose. They either believed they could not trust anyone enough or feared that any attempt or failed intervention could lead to worse consequences. They feared that interventions might cause them to be separated from their siblings, that they may be abused worse in foster care, and that their parents would be sent to jail. They assumed their family life would be seriously disrupted or that their disclosure would ruin their family's reputation. Several discussed there being no point, that no one would help them. They felt trapped or worried their abuse would be too hard for others to handle.

Feelings of isolation and hopelessness were common. Likewise, each reported strong feelings of shame, guilt or confusion that deterred their disclosure. Several reported they were confused about their sexuality after their abuse. More than half of the men worried they might get into trouble if they told someone about the abuse, and blamed themselves for having failed to prevent or stop it. Some said their abuse was so normalized that they either thought what was happening was normal, or believed that it was their role in life to be used as a sex object.

Approximately half indicated that their previous lack of knowledge or understanding (in regard to the impact of their abuse) or a lack of awareness (that they were in fact victims of sexual abuse) were barriers to their disclosure. Nearly three-quarters wanted to protect their parents' reputation or to protect their parents from information they believed would be too hard for them to handle. They lived with a sense of hopelessness and isolation, eagerly anticipating when they would be old enough to get away from their abusers.

Several said that they had been physically aroused during the abuse, despite their lack of willingness and consent. They recalled having been paralyzed with fear when first approached by their abuser(s), then confused by their subsequent arousal and ejaculation. Despite this, only a few discussed feeling worried about being labelled as "homosexual" or feared that their abuse may have made them gay. Most felt strongly that their abuse had not affected their sexuality.

Jacob was confused about his ability to engage in sexual relations with his mother. Two others who were abused by their mothers were confused by loving comments their mothers made to them during their abuse. These males also believed that since their fathers didn't help them, no one else was likely to help them either. These barriers highlight the considerable struggles males face when dealing with sexual abuse. Overall, they beg answers to the following questions:

How Did These Men Perceive Others Would React if They Did Disclose?

It's important to understand that when these boys and men considered disclosing their abuse, they first thought about the possible responses of those they would disclose to. Many worried they would be judged or viewed differently. Some feared they would be considered perverted, crazy or seen as future predators. These fears overpowered their desire to disclose.

How Did Their Negative Perceptions of Others Make Them React?

The anticipated negative responses of others acted as a strong deterrent to seeking help. Several internalized their parents' lack of capacity to support them and thought of themselves as unworthy, unlovable, responsible for the abuse, damaged, broken, or otherwise flawed. They coped by either dissociating, isolating, avoiding, or attempting to numb themselves from the pain. Others buried their memories and often tolerated further abuse.

Most were too overwhelmed with emotions of fear and thoughts of not being believed or of being abandoned. They worried that exposing their experiences of abuse, intimate thoughts, and vulnerabilities to another person would completely destroy them, and they made the decision to survive by maintaining their silence. Most waited to disclose until adulthood, when they felt stronger, more supported, and less reliant on others for emotional, physical, and financial support.

Conversely, some chose to rewrite their memories and view their abuse as less distressing than it was. They added elements of personal choice to their memories (though no choice had existed) or made the decision not to think about the abuse at all, building emotional walls around experiences too painful to share.

Why Did They Wait So Long?

The men in my research waited between one and 59 years to discuss their abuse with anyone else. A few waited because of memory loss; others were simply too traumatized. A majority remained silent in part because they were confused about their degree of participation and feared being blamed or rejected. They also feared for their safety or were completely dependent on their abusers; some believed no one could help them.

A majority of the men reported feeling shame and guilt for having been physiologically aroused, for not stopping their abuse sooner, or for being a burden to their families. To avoid feelings of shame, some withdrew from friends and family. Others withdrew out of fear they might accidentally disclose. A few drank or used illicit drugs to help them forget their abuse and waited years to make their eventual disclosure. Some remained silent because they feared it would be too much for them to bear or didn't realize how badly their abuse had affected them.

While each of these reasons for not disclosing their experiences of childhood sexual abuse was valid for them at the time, their reasons changed as they matured. Eventually, each did make a disclosure to someone prior to participating in this research.

Name	Age when abuse began	Age when abuse ended	Sexually abused more than once?	Sexually abused by more than one person?
Aaron	15	15	Yes	Yes
Allen	8	14	Yes	Yes
Anthony	2.5	11	Yes	Yes
Garrett	2	18	Yes	Yes
Gordon	5	12	Yes	Yes
Jacob	3.5	13	Yes	Yes
Josh	8	10	Yes	Yes
Julien	16	30	Yes	Yes
Leon	13	17	Yes	Yes
Leonard	3.5	11	Yes	Yes
Michael	13	13	No	No
Phillip	14	14	Yes	Yes
Ricky	5	14	Yes	Yes

What Prompted Them to Finally Tell Someone About Their Abuse?

Participants in my research had many different reasons for why, when and where they finally did disclose. Just under half made disclosures after they became more physically mature and were well established as independent adults and in supportive relationships. Some disclosed when they reached adulthood and became parents themselves. Others shared when they felt the need to be understood by someone else, were faced with a crisis, or were forced to stop using self-destructive coping mechanisms. A few made disclosures because they felt like they might implode or take their own lives if they didn't. One disclosed to his brother unintentionally because he thought his brother already knew.

Several admitted they had begun seeing therapists for reasons other than their abuse, and that they disclosed their abuse only after years of learning to trust their therapists. These findings, including the delays in disclosing their abuse, highlight how difficult it can be for boys and men—even when they are seeking help— to discuss their experiences of abuse for the first time.

Male Reluctance to Seek Help

Prior to conducting my research, there was relatively little research that examined why boys and men seldom report abuse.

In 1980, a clinical social worker named Maria Nasjleti examined the reasons why boys in the USA, aged 12 to 17 who were known to be victims of incest did not disclose. Nasjleti was among the first to recognize that male victims had been virtually ignored. Looking at the experiences of nine boys who were dependents of the court and ordered to participate in therapy, she observed an "extreme resistance" to discussing their abuse. Most simply wanted to forget it ever happened and refused to discuss their feelings. Nasjleti explained that at the time, both the public and professionals didn't think sexual abuse had a significant impact on men and boys. She said, some people believed that the "seduction of a male child" was a "positive sexual experience for the boy."[114]

In 2005, in another study, Dr. Ramona Alaggia, Chair of Children's Mental Health at the University of Toronto, interviewed 30 victims of childhood sexual abuse (participants were both male and female). She found the overall trend for both men and women was to delay disclosure. More than half (58 percent) waited to disclose until well into adulthood, though many had made indirect attempts that included verbal statements about not wanting to be left alone with the abuser and requests that their non-abusive parent stay home from work. Those who held back from disclosing usually did so until they had emotional breakdowns later in life. The men reported feeling profound isolation. They believed that males were rarely victimized and that they would be viewed as homosexual if they disclosed. The fear they might somehow become abusers themselves also caused them to remain silent.[115]

In 2008, researchers Lynn Sorsoli, Maryam Kia-Keating, and Frances Grossman interviewed 16 men who were victims of childhood sexual abuse about their disclosure experiences. They explored to whom disclosures were made, experiences of disclosure, and the incentives and barriers they faced. Their results revealed very few actual experiences of disclosure and many barriers. Only one out of the 16 men had deliberately disclosed the full extent of his abuse, and when he did, the results were "disastrous"—he wasn't believed. Others had attempted to tell the truth about their abuse, but their disclosures were incomplete or minimized and often cryptic.[116] Their partial disclosures, too, were met with disbelief or simply not acknowledged. "The stark reality is that these men's initial attempts to tell were neither well received nor encouraged,"[117] concluded the researchers.

Similar to the results of my study, some of the men in Sorsoli, Kia-Keating, and Grossman's study feared that disclosures would only make their situations worse. Others believed that they would not get the help they needed since someone had already known they were being abused and did nothing, leaving them with the impression that abuse was acceptable or normal. Others found it hard to believe that their abuse went undetected. Some felt it would be too hard for others to hear about the abuse, feared being considered homosexual, or feared being thought of as a potential offender. Two had been able to disclose their physical abuse but not their sexual abuse.

Some indicated that biases regarding masculinity—for example, that it is culturally unacceptable for men to be victims—kept them from discussing their experiences. They believed that disclosing was something they should never do unless it was to someone they had known and trusted for many years. In these cases, their fear of negative repercussions outweighed their desire to disclose. "These men actually seemed caught in a double bind," the researchers concluded. They experienced shame and felt reluctant to share their histories "while simultaneously expressing shame for not telling earlier."[118]

Other researchers have examined the social construction of masculinity and how it affects help-seeking behavior. They have discovered that even as adults, men are less likely than women to seek help for problems they see as unusual, especially if they view themselves as deviant and the problem as central to their identity. Men also are unlikely to seek help if they perceive that other men endorse norms of self-reliance. Generally, they perceive the risk as too great in proportion to the help they might receive.[119]

Additionally, if the majority of their peers have never mentioned having a similar problem, or if their peers regularly make statements about the importance of being strong and not letting things get to them, victimized men are more likely to remain silent and deny their own feelings of vulnerability and weakness. Similarly, if a man sees himself as possessing similar qualities as his peers, he won't want to be rejected for seeking help.

Although research indicates that male childhood sexual abuse continues to remain underreported to authorities, poorly recognized by clinicians,[120] and undertreated in adulthood,[121] studies on disclosure reveal that a reluctance to seek help is not exclusive to males. One researcher estimated that 30 to 80 percent of all victims purposefully don't disclose before adulthood;[122] however, it's impossible to produce reliable data on disclosure since silence cannot be measured.

Some theories offer insight into understanding the processes involved in both male and female disclosure.[123] Approach and avoidance factors have been suggested as influencing a person's decision to disclose. Victims also will assess their supports. If they believe that the risks outweigh possible benefits, they won't disclose,[124] which suggests that disclosure is not a single event, but a process of weighing what is at stake. Social exchange theory proposes that on the one hand, disclosing sometimes can stop victimization. Conversely, it can lead to secondary trauma, such as being blamed or disbelieved.[125]

More recently, in 2011, Dr. Sally Hunter from the School of Rural Medicine at the University of England conducted a study on the process of disclosure. She interviewed 22 male and female survivors of childhood sexual abuse, and learned that only five had purposefully disclosed and that each had experienced some form of disclosure-related trauma. They either were not believed or supported or their situation did not improve. Four of the participants also described the ways they had acted out in hopes that someone would identify they were in distress.[126]

Although her results were not differentiated by gender, Hunter identified the barriers to disclosure as lack of positive family environment, culture, fear of punishment, fear the abuser would move on to other victims, fear of what might happen within the family, fear of not being believed, feelings of responsibility, self-blame, shameful feelings about homosexuality and fear of being labeled as homosexual. One victim feared her father might kill her perpetrator, then be sent to jail. Another feared what would happen to her mother if her father left the family. Similar to what was found in my research, anger in adulthood became a strong motivator for eventual disclosure. They felt anger toward their offending parent for abusing them, and toward their non-offending parent for failing to protect them. Men made selective disclosures, telling their intimate partner, a friend, or a therapist, while women revealed their abuse to a family member or the police.

Dr. Hunter also recognized disclosure as a lifelong process. Many of her participants viewed their lives in terms of pre- and post-disclosure. As adults, some sought justice after they became less fearful and understood that they could be protected by the police. Over time, it also became easier for them to talk about their experiences as children. Some also shared their stories with family members and, unfortunately, even as adults, experienced negative consequences for having done so.

In 2005, Tine Jensen, Wenke Gulbrandsen, Svein Mossige, Sissel Reichelt, and Odd Arne Tjersland investigated the contexts in which children were able to disclose sexual abuse.[127] Their study showed that male children typically found it too difficult to find situations that provided either enough privacy or the supportive prompts needed for them to disclose. Participants said that since they were never directly questioned about being abused, they never felt it was the "right time" to discuss it. They said that it was too difficult to get time alone with their chosen confidant and they were sensitive to potential reactions. They worried their disclosures would be misinterpreted or that their abuse experiences would be trivialized.

This tells us that when certain conditions are not met, such as privacy, support, and proper prompting, then opportunities for disclosure may be missed. If people continue to fail to recognize that boys and men may be victims, these individuals may be left with the feeling that they are an anomaly, that they are unworthy of help, or that no one would be willing to help.

Getting Help

Fortunately, all of the men I interviewed were seeking help. Below is some of what they said about their experience of getting help.

Allen, who initially attended therapy only to appease his wife, found it beneficial. He learned to accept that the abuse he endured was not his fault and that he was not "f***ed in the head."

"Talking with other men who experienced similar abuse was powerful," he said. "It showed me I don't own the shame."

Despite his initial fears, Aaron said discussing his abuse has been empowering. "The power victims have over their offenders is speaking up," he said. "What boys and men have to understand is that it takes courage to come forward. It takes true courage to stand up and say, 'Yes, this happened to me. We have a voice now!'"

Josh felt the same way after facing his abuse.

"I know that I am stronger. I think if I had understood what it could do to my life, I might have said something sooner. I wouldn't have wasted my life. I can take the energy and make it into something I can heal from, and I can let it make me stronger."

When Jacob disclosed to his therapist, he told her he didn't want to relive every memory.

"I told her up front, 'Look, I've been through this before. I don't want to relive every memory.' She told me, 'Modern therapy doesn't make you relive all of your past. We'll discuss what you want to discuss.' She was very good, one of the best. We focused on tools to deal with the flashbacks and stress."

Anthony's experience helped him feel less isolated.

"There's a normalizing effect, you know, my story isn't like everybody else's. No two stories are exactly the same, but I don't feel as separate, as different. I found a group of men I can relate to and who can relate to me."

Michael shared a metaphor about attending therapy:

"Do you know what the buffalo do when a storm is coming? Buffalo turn and walk into the storm. They don't try to outrun it, they don't try to avoid it, and they don't stand still. They move toward the storm. They instinctively know that if they head into it, they will come out the other side much faster than if they were to try and outrun it or just sit still."

PART 4

IDENTIFYING CHILD SEXUAL ABUSE

The reality is that unless you are a medical doctor examining a child and looking for sexual trauma, or the child discloses, you aren't likely to know for sure if abuse has occurred. Children who are groomed, threatened, afraid, confused, worried, ashamed, or feeling responsible for being abused are not likely to talk about it. However, they may begin to display symptoms, including a sudden extreme change in their character, or they may express their distress in other ways. It's important to be aware of common trauma responses.

Common Emotional, Behavior, Cognitive, and Physiological Responses to Trauma

Emotionally, many abused children feel anger toward the people who harmed them and toward those who failed to protect them. They may also feel anger at themselves. "Young children, by virtue of their level of cognitive development, attribute everything that happens to their own actions or their own magical thinking."[128] They have difficulty seeing other people's contributions to their circumstances and feel responsible for the abuse and for the subsequent problems they have no control over. Worry about their own mental instability may cause them to decompensate (regress emotionally) and develop negative core beliefs about themselves.[129]

Behaviorally, after experiencing abuse, children can experience dysregulation in many different ways. Some become shy and withdrawn, while others become bullies.[130] Others develop learning difficulties and are subject to social rejection. Many experience negative repercussions because of behavioral problems they express while attempting to avoid distressing memories or while dysregulated. When children have been victimized, their consequent behavior often makes them easy targets for further abuse from their peers, including bullying and rejection.

Sexually abused children may engage in sexual acts with other children or display anger, rage, threatening behavior, extreme fearlessness or acting out.[131] Ricky, for instance, came home and tore apart the drum set he previously loved.

Sexually abused boys can have extremely difficult times during both childhood and adolescence. Although most youth display some out-of-character behavioral changes as they hit developmental milestones, severe manifestations must be recognized as possible signs of abuse. When these changes occur during the course of normal maturation they often are not recognized, or are misattributed by parents.

Cognitively, in a similar way to the experiences of female victims, male victims may come to view themselves as damaged goods, unworthy of being loved.[132] Many develop low self-esteem, a distorted self-image, and a diminished sense of self-worth. Following sexual trauma a victim's view of himself and the world around him is never the same. His views must now be reconstructed to include the trauma. His age, previous life experiences, and present supports will profoundly affect the interpretation of, or meaning he places on the traumatic event(s).

Many victims blame themselves for the abuse. They do so in part because assuming a level of responsibility allows them to maintain the illusion that they had a level of control during the abuse and therefore have control of future events. They prefer this to facing the reality that they were completely vulnerable and helpless. This illusion allows them to maintain their *internal locus of control*—the feeling that *they* have control over the outcome of events in their world. Many children abused by their parents blame themselves in part to hold on to their parental relations and the idea that their parents are somewhat decent and good people. They have to, for the alternative—that their parents are bad people and they are stuck with them—is too scary.

Early Experiences and the Development of Attachment Styles

Early experiences in life lay the foundation and become the lens through which children (and later adults) see themselves, others and the world around them. The "view" children establish in their youth becomes their blueprint or "internal working model,"[133] from which they develop their ability to "attach" or be in close relationship with others. Youth and adults make decisions about whether or not others are safe and can be trusted, whether or not they believe themselves to be worthy of receiving love, and whether or not the world is a safe place, based on their early environment and life experiences.

In adulthood this lens is referred to as *attachment style*. Early research conducted by Mary D. Salter Ainsworth, Mary C. Blehar, Everett Waters, and Sally N. Wall identified three distinct attachment styles that emerge based on a child's early experiences, including parental rearing and other environmental factors.[134] These attachment styles have since been expanded and refined into the following categories (though different authors and researchers categorize them differently):

- People with *secure attachment* generally believe that they are worthy of love and capable of both giving and receiving the love they desire.[135] They also believe that the world is a relatively safe place to live. They are capable of intimacy and not overly insecure nor overly jealous.[136]

- People with *anxious attachment* struggle with insecurity. They are plagued with a highly active sensitivity to any perceived threat to the safety or availability of their relationship. These people fear small issues will end relationships and tend to need a lot of reassurance. They jump to conclusions easily, doubt their own worthiness, and struggle to trust others.[137]

- Those with an *avoidant attachment* style may see themselves as more of a free spirit. They see relationships as a threat to their independence and generally feel very alone, even in relationships. Although they desire close intimate relations, they fear them. Many hold out for the ideal relationship and believe that most others are unwilling, unreliable or incapable of meeting their needs. They work hard to keep intimacy at a safe distance. Avoidants believe they must survive on their own and generally have an escape plan in mind.[138] Hollywood makes millions out of romanticizing these types.

- Adults with an *ambivalent attachment* style are people pleasers who play it safe and mold themselves to meet the expectations of others. Although they may fluctuate between strong emotions of love and hate, they hide their own negative emotions. Because they deny their own needs, and don't ask for much, they are never really sure where they stand with others. They see others as capable of meeting their needs but likely to abandon them if they really get to know them.[139] They live in fear of being abandoned or rejected.

- *Disorganized attachment* is a combination of insecure and avoidant attachment styles. People with this attachment style have a negative view of themselves and others. They want close attachment but don't trust it and are not confident they deserve it. They may push people away to avoid being hurt.

In general terms, people with secure attachment most often come from parent-toddler relations where the parent or parents were sufficiently responsive, nurturing and predictable. Ambivalent children may have grown up wondering if their parents loved them and walking on eggshells. Their parents may have used the cold shoulder or avoidance as a means to control their behaviors.[140] Both avoidant and disorganized attachment styles are indicative of infants or toddlers with a significant history of abuse, neglect or extreme chaos. The good or bad news about these attachment styles is that they can be changed. Anxious and avoidant types can learn to become secure, but unfortunately secure types may also develop more insecure styles if they are significantly betrayed or traumatized.

ATTACHMENT INJURY

Children, youth and adults who were once securely attached but then are abused, abandoned or betrayed commonly suffer what is referred to as *attachment injury,* which is essentially a crisis of trust.[141]

The human brain is continually modified by its experiences, good and bad. Because the brain controls emotional regulation and is highly dependent on its environment, infants and children who experience traumatic events, and have not yet learned to self-regulate, often become emotionally and physiologically dysregulated. Traumatic experiences that occur when a child's self-regulatory skills have not yet developed more rigorously impact children over the long term. The impact of sexual trauma on any victim depends in part on their pre-trauma ability to self-regulate, as well as their resources before, during and after traumatic events occur. Traumatic memories are either integrated and then stored as an unfortunate event of the past, or they begin to lead a life of their own.

"Despite the human capacity to survive and adapt, traumatic experiences can alter people's psychological, biological and social equilibrium to such a degree that the memory of one particular event comes to taint all their other experiences."[142]

As the brain tries to protect trauma victims from reliving their harmful events, it also uses information about those past experiences to influence how new stimuli are processed. Trauma victims are especially sensitive to new stimuli because they may signal either a danger or an opportunity. A victim living with hypervigilance, hyperarousal, and the inability to self-soothe can quickly deem new stimuli to be unsafe and a stress-response will be triggered (trauma responses are described in the next section).

Although responses to being triggered and traumatized vary, two common yet extreme neurobiological responses frequently occur instantaneously during sexual assaults: *tonic immobility* and *dissociation*.[143]

Tonic immobility is essentially freezing. A victim may become physically immobile or lose their ability to move in response to extreme fear. Logic and instinct dictate that when danger is imminent, and people believe they have the time and ability to either fight or defend themselves or flee (escape), they will. But if victims don't believe they have the time or capacity to fight or flee, and they believe their assailants will overpower them, they may become paralyzed.[144] Their muscles may become rigid, as if they are dead or frozen. In these moments time may feel as if it has slowed down, and they may dissociate.

Dissociation is a neurobiological response that protects us when physical fight or flight doesn't seem possible in situations that evoke fear or terror.[145] While it may look like someone is dazed or zoned out, this reaction "prepares" a victim for mental or physical injury. During dissociation the brain releases pleasure-producing endogenous opioids that allow the body to handle both the physical and emotional pain it expects to endure.[146] These naturally produced chemicals, in effect, lessen the short-term, immediate impact of trauma.

People who dissociate report a sense of disconnection, "unreality" or numbness similar to being on drugs.[147] Victims experiencing mild to moderate dissociation often report experiencing a sense of depersonalization, or a lack of familiarity with themselves or their surroundings. They may look in the mirror and fail to recognize themselves, or feel as if life is passing them by, as if they aren't really present or fully participating in reality.

More severely dissociated people sometimes report an experience of hovering above the trauma (with a sense of distance), watching it as if it were happening to someone else. Although dissociation helps victims to survive in the short term, it becomes problematic if relied upon or used too frequently over a long period of time. Victims who dissociate often develop a subconscious tendency to use this response even during benign situations when they are triggered.

Dissociation can be extremely dangerous if it occurs while driving or walking in busy areas. It also can make it difficult to engage in and pay attention to important tasks at school, at work or in social settings. Dissociation can persist long after the trauma has ended or it can happen for the first time years after the trauma occurred.[148]

Triggers

As human beings our brains continually process signals or stimuli that can trigger or spark memories. Triggers are any stimuli that remind victims, either consciously or unconsciously, of traumatic events.[149] They are activated through any one or more of our five senses (sight, sound, touch, taste and smell).

Visual triggers, for instance, might include seeing a place that reminds a victim of where they were abused, or seeing someone who resembles their abuser in any way (e.g., the same hairstyle, clothing, or way of walking). Male children who were abused by their fathers and grow up to look like their fathers report being triggered by their own reflections in the mirror.

Audible triggers are sounds that remind victims of their abuse. This may include phrases or words used by their abuser (e.g., "You're so special"). Hearing about someone else's abuse, in person or on the TV or radio, also may be triggering.

Olfactory triggers are smells that resemble odors sensed before, during or after abuse experiences. Examples may include the smell of cologne, alcohol, cigarette smoke or bodily excretions that remind them of their abuser.

Sensory triggers include any physical touch that reminds them of the abuse or grooming behaviors used prior to their abuse. A victim might be triggered during dental work if they have been orally violated in the past. For some victims, having an accelerated heart rate may remind them of their trauma, since they experienced it during their abuse. Using exercise as a coping mechanism may become challenging, if not impossible, until they are successfully treated.

Taste triggers may include anything that conjures a taste memory related to the victim's abuse experience. Examples include certain foods, sexual excretions, alcohol or tobacco.

Triggers are very personal. Different things trigger different people depending on their experiences. As such, they are often difficult to identify. Triggers can also *generalize* or transfer, causing victims to begin to see benign or nonthreatening stimuli as threatening. A victim who initially was triggered by the sight of someone who reminded him of his offender—for example, a tall, gray-haired man with a mustache—may later find himself triggered by all tall men with mustaches, no matter what their hair color. Triggers can become increasingly subtle or generalize if left untreated.[150]

Many people experience being triggered without being able to make sense of what is happening to them or knowing what has triggered them. Understandably, being triggered can lead boys and men to act in ways that make no sense to themselves or others unless they are aware of trauma responses and their trauma histories.[151] The experience of being triggered is distressing and may cause victims to engage in bizarre behaviors, such as fleeing a restaurant without explanation, declining further social invitations, or getting upset for no apparent reason. Triggers often lead victims to engage in avoidant behaviors, which can lead to isolation and loneliness.

Rumination

Following a traumatic event the human brain automatically tries to restore itself to a state of equilibrium.[152] While doing so, it may subject itself to small doses of events, those that are not yet resolved, in an attempt to resolve or make sense of them.[153] Many people engage in purposeful rumination with the intent of better understanding their problems. However, attempting to logically understand or "solve" abuse can be maladaptive, since reason can't solve the problem of having been abused.[154] Victims could spend a considerable amount of time and energy ruminating about why they were abused or what they could have done differently when, in fact, they are not responsible for their abuse.

Rumination also appears to predict the onset, severity, and maintenance of depressive states and interferes with a person's problem-solving capacities.[155] It may cause victims to rewrite their original scripts—namely, to change their memories from the truth that they were completely traumatized and helpless, to a response-memory where they had a degree of willingness and control.[156]

How the Brain Responds to Stress

Being repeatedly exposed to high levels of stress can impact the brain's physical structure, size and ability to function properly. Increased and persistently high levels of cortisol, the hormone produced during stressful events, physiologically increases the number of neural connections in the brain's fear center, making victims become hypersensitive to stress. At the same time, these increased cortisol levels cause the areas of the brain responsible for stress management to deteriorate. There is a great YouTube video called *How Stress Affects Your Brain* by Madhumita Murgia that describes this process.[157] It's worth the 4.5 minutes it takes to watch.

While most adults have established at least some biological and psychological coping mechanisms to assist them in recovering from traumatic events, children may not yet have these in place. If abuse occurs before they have learned to self-regulate the aftereffects can be catastrophic.

A victim's ability to cope with abuse and their resulting symptoms is impacted by their age, temperament, developmental stage, and whether or not they have learned to self-regulate. It is also impacted by the availability of resources, both pre- and post-abuse, the social context in which their abuse occurred, and their interpretation of the abuse.[158] It also depends on their relationship to the perpetrator, whether the perpetrator used violence or grooming techniques, the severity of the abuse, and whether it was an isolated incident or ongoing.[159] Research has also shown that the number and complexity of symptoms children suffer increase as the number and types of traumatic stressors increase.[160]

Although experiencing any one of the previously described trauma response symptoms is challenging, more commonly, at least two or more symptoms coexist in persons who have experienced trauma. Numerous studies of childhood maltreatment reveal that interpersonal traumas place children at risk of developing coexisting problems, including anxiety, depression, mood disorders, disruptive behavior disorders, or pathologies such as dissociative identity disorder, PTSD, and clinical depression.[161] The likelihood of a secondary disorder developing increases as the number of traumatic stressors increase.[162]

Children who previously have been able to regulate themselves may regress after experiencing abuse and develop sleep problems. Out of a need to adapt to having been traumatized the "growing brain organizes itself to be more reactive to survival functioning at the expense of developing the areas of the brain which are responsible for the modulation of impulse control and emotional regulation."[163] Being unable to soothe themselves, children with an already dysregulated stress response may begin to live in anticipation of the next threat. They may become increasingly unable to pay attention or concentrate on nonthreatening stimuli. These children are often deemed to be problematic and misdiagnosed as having attention deficit/hyperactivity disorder, whereas they need first to be understood as victims of trauma.[164] Traumatized youth may become increasingly uninterested in the nonthreatening stimuli that other children find enjoyable. Many abuse victims discover that the only way to feel safe is by isolating themselves.[165]

Experiencing shame has a particularly disruptive interpersonal impact because it often leaves victims feeling judged by others. To avoid feeling shame and judgement many victims withdraw socially, or become meek and submissive. Living in isolation becomes problematic in and of itself. It prevents them from taking healthy risks and establishing healthy relations. It also leaves them at high risk for being bullied, experiencing further victimization, and developing depression. Living in isolation becomes the self-fulfilling prophecy, the proof that they are not worthy of love. Experiencing childhood sexual abuse can significantly alter the trajectory of an entire life.[166]

Youth and adults who experience trauma and trauma response symptoms may come to see themselves as defective, different, inferior, unattractive, used or rejected.[167] In response, some become angry and rebel, or build emotional walls around the experiences that are too painful to bear.

OPPOSITIONAL DEFIANT DISORDER AND CONDUCT DISORDER

Youth who display patterns of deliberately argumentative, vindictive, angry, disruptive, and defiant behavior toward authority figures are sometimes diagnosed as oppositionally defiant when the behavior patterns persist for more than six months. These behaviors may manifest in one or more of their current environments (e.g., home, school, work, social group), with symptoms generally first appearing during preschool.[168]

When behaviors become more severe, last for a period of at least 12 months, and include physical aggression toward people or animals, the destruction of property, patterns of theft, deceit, or forcing others to engage in sexual activity, a diagnosis of conduct disorder may apply. Children diagnosed with oppositional defiant disorder and conduct disorder often come from environments of harsh, neglectful or inconsistent parenting.

Two of the men who participated in my research turned to alcohol to numb themselves. As adults, using alcohol or sustaining the means of obtaining drugs as a means to cope can easily snowball and lead to convictions or further diagnoses.

Although many boys and men who have been abused go on to lead healthy and productive lives and to function well despite their histories, it does not mean their trauma had no impact.[169]

As an organ, the human brain is continually modified, and what a person feels in the present also influences how they see and recall the past.[170] If an adult develops depression, for instance, it will influence how he recalls previous memories. Men who rewrite their past are not likely to see themselves as victims, perhaps contributing to the reasons their abuse goes undetected. Another reason is people's emotional desire or inability to be confident that they see abuse. This is discussed below.

Willful Blindness

In her book *Willful Blindness: Why We Ignore the Obvious at Our Peril*, author Margaret Heffernan explains that every day, significant numbers of intelligent people unconsciously choose to be ignorant of things that are true on a daily basis because the reality or consequences of that truth would be too devastating.[171] Heffernan explains that people aren't necessarily consciously choosing to avoid truth; but rather, that certain neurological processes take place in the brain that contribute to keeping people willfully blind.

Heffernan references research by Dr. Robert Burton, author of *On Being Certain: Believing You Are Right Even When You Are Not* and former chief of neurology at USCF Medical Center at Mount Zion Hospital in San Francisco.[172] Burton examined how neural networks in the human brain are wired, reporting there are physical components that act as biases in our brain. We are wired to reject information that will make us less certain. When faced with conflict, neurons in our brain actually activate our defense mechanisms of avoidance, denial, minimization, trivialization and so on. These neurons literally work to shut down negative thoughts by engaging in faulty reasoning. Our brains then recruit reward neurons to make us feel good about our faulty decisions.

Heffernan also references studies conducted by neuroscientists from the University of London who report that falling in love actually activates areas of the brain associated with receiving reward, while simultaneously deactivating areas associated with alertness, memory and negative emotions. This could be why people in love often ignore warning signs and seek out like-minded people to reassure them of their optimism. The reassurance they receive then further narrows their attention and leaves them with blind spots.

Blatant examples of willful blindness occur when people ignore health risks and engage in risky behaviors. It also occurs in the corporate world when organizations prioritize growth and profit over moral accountability. In their pursuit of money and power they engage in wrongful acts or omissions, with little or no regard for destructive consequences to others or the environment.

Perhaps the most damaging examples of willful blindness are committed by adults who ignore signs of their children being groomed or sexually abused. Heffernan provides the example of a mother who observed her husband having an erection after reading to their ten-year-old daughter. When she confronted him, he denied it, so she told herself that she must have been seeing things. After all, if she was right, it would most certainly mean the end of her marriage, financial security, and sense of family. Later, when the child's doctor informed her that her daughter displayed signs of sexual abuse, the mother recalled what she had previously decided to ignore—her husband's erection and the fact that her husband had stopped having intercourse with her two years prior.

Any parent who suspects their partner may have an unhealthy interest in one of their children should investigate those instincts. Ignoring them could have catastrophic results for children who are vulnerable to abuse.

Why Good People Don't Act

There are a number of reasons why responsible adults fail to act when they suspect a child is being abused:

- Getting involved may feel uncomfortable and could be a lengthy process.

- They worry about the consequences of getting involved.

- They comfort themselves with the idea that they must be wrong.

- They rationalize to themselves that someone else will help. This is called the "bystander effect" or diffusion of responsibility.

- They know the alleged offender and believe that person to be incapable of abuse.

- They believe the child is capable of asking for help should they need it.

- They don't believe anything like this would or could ever happen in their environment or to anyone they know.

PART 5

WHAT ADULTS CAN DO TO PREVENT ABUSE OR DETECT IT SOONER

Based on what some of the men I spoke to reported, it is clear that in *some* instances, having some basic knowledge of grooming and sexual abuse may have helped prevent their abuse or it may have helped to end it sooner. **My intention here is not to suggest that the burden of preventing abuse ever be placed on children. Instead, I am highlighting the important role that adults can play in abuse prevention and early detection.** Having more information-based discussions with youth and young adults may increase the likelihood of keeping them safe. Given that many people may be unsure of what to say and when, here are a few ideas:

What to Do with Infants and Youth

- Start talking to them early about the "private parts" of the human body. Include details of each sex as early as possible. Use the proper names: penis, bum or anus, vagina, and breasts. If you can't use these words with them, they likely won't feel comfortable using them with you.

- Tell them that these are private parts that other people are not allowed to touch, except in case of a medical emergency. Discuss who (teachers or daycare workers) is allowed to help them in the washroom if they need help.

- Explain to them that they can and should say "no" or "stop" if someone tries to take off their underwear, touch their private parts, or make them touch someone else's private parts. Also, explain that they need to tell you if someone tries to do this.

- Explain that it is not just strangers who might try to touch them, that sometimes it is a family member or friend, and that does not make it right. Explain that "games" that involve things like touching and taking their clothes off are not allowed.

- Make sure children understand they are not in trouble for talking openly to you about their private parts or incidents that happen.

As you do talk to your children allow them to ask questions and answer them honestly. Control your own feelings of discomfort when you talk to them about sex and when they ask tough questions. Remember shame is learned. As adults we understand the meaning and intention behind wrongful acts. Infants and children don't and that is fine. But, children need knowledge, language and permission to discuss abuse. They do need to know that if someone tries to touch their genitals inappropriately it's wrong, and they need to tell you. Perpetrators may reason that if the child knows how to say 'no', they also may know to tell their parents if something does happen, revealing them as a potential abuser.

If discussing abuse sounds terrifying, a great book to read to infants and young children is *Talk About Touch* by Sandy Kleven (available for under $20 on Amazon).[173] This book says it all. It provides a great example of how to explain bad touch to infants and children.

Leonard said he would have spoken up much sooner if he'd known about bad touch. He believes that if the child psychologist he'd seen in kindergarten had asked him more direct probing questions, he likely would have disclosed his abuse. But he had no idea why the psychologist wanted to talk to him.

"If you don't ask pointed questions, [a child] can miss it," said Leonard. "Yes, I understand you are leading them, but children sometimes don't think about it. I see this with my daughter with her homework. I'll ask her, 'Do you have homework?' She'll say, "No.' Then I say, 'Are you sure? I thought you had some math homework.' Then it's 'oh yeah.' If you don't say 'math' they don't even think about it." Leonard believes his psychologist and teacher suspected something, but neither asked him directly if anything was wrong. "The system is flawed," he said.

What Not to Do with Infants and Youth

- Don't send verbal messages that they are not to discuss sex or sex-related issues. Don't say, "We don't talk about sex [or another sexual matter] in this house" or "no one likes a tattletale." If you want to teach this be sure to make it clear that reporting bad touch is not considered tattling.

- Don't send the message that you are too busy or have too many problems to handle their issues. Make it clear that you are available and willing to listen and help at all times, regardless of personal or professional circumstances. Several of my participants reported they felt their abuse would have been too much for their parents to handle.

- Don't force your children to hug or kiss people if they don't want to. Forcing them to do otherwise sends a mixed message that their body really is not their own. Allow your children to decide if they feel safe to hug and kiss the people you bring into their life, including people you know. This reinforces the idea that they are allowed to set healthy boundaries for themselves, even with trusted friends. If they can't say no when their parents are present, they may not feel comfortable saying no when they aren't.

- Don't force your kids to take your word for who is safe and who isn't. Allow them to have input. They may have more information than you do. If they don't like someone with whom you've allowed them to be alone, ask for more details.

- Don't minimize your children's concerns about being alone with older children and adults. Ask probing questions if your children tell you they don't like certain people or don't want to be alone with them. Ask them why. If they say they don't like the games they play, get them to describe the games.

What to Do with Youth and Pre-Teens

- Allow them to attend sex education classes and/or teach them basic information about their bodies, reproduction, sex and masturbation. This is important even for families wanting to maintain rules about abstinence. Teach youth that by definition, masturbation is a solo sport, and they do not need anyone to teach them how it's done. If they don't hear about it from you they will learn about it somewhere else. If you teach them about it while they are young enough, they may even believe the idea to be gross, but they won't feel shocked, entitled, or deprived if an older teen or adult tries to introduce it to them as a grooming tactic.

- Create a safe space to have these sex talks. Let them know there is something important you want to discuss with them. If needed, take them fishing, for walks, out for meals, or for a country drive. Start the conversation and get it flowing before you introduce the subject.

- Educate them openly about grooming tactics (that people may be nice to children, but they are not always nice people, and if someone "changes" they can tell you).
- Discuss with them early the value of not engaging in sexual acts while they are young.

If they disclose abuse, invite them to keep talking, reassure them that it's not their fault and seek professional help. Aaron said he wished he had known more about abuse when he was a child.

"If I knew that grooming involves someone giving you alcohol before you're allowed to have it, or letting you drive their car without your parents' permission, or letting you look at dirty pictures, or pays you special attention; if I knew that kind of stuff even existed when I was a kid, then maybe I would have been a little leery about letting what happened happen," he said. Aaron may not have been successful at warding off his abuse, but he most likely would have felt less confused and responsible if he'd have known he was being abused.

All this being said, more information is not always enough. It would not have helped boys like Jacob, Leonard, Anthony or Garrett, who were abused by their parents from infancy.

What Not to Do with Youth and Pre-Teens

- If you see something that causes concern, or if your teen has started displaying extreme changes in their character or behavior, don't ignore it or chalk it up to a change in hormones.

- Don't ignore your instincts if you suspect something is wrong. Probe and ask questions.

- When asking questions, don't imply by your words or body language that they may be responsible if something has happened.

- Don't ask questions in a manner that contains the answer you would like to hear. For instance, don't say, "You're okay, right?" This may signal to them that you can't handle the truth or that there is only one answer you want to hear. Instead, say, "It seems like something is wrong." This way creates more room for an open and honest answer.

- If they won't talk to you, find out who they will talk to (for example a trusted aunt or other trusted friend or sibling) and seek their help or seek professional help.

Teachers and Other Helping Professionals

If you are a teacher, coach or other professional who works with children, check in with any children who are isolating, frequently bruised, wearing the same clothes day after day, being bullied, frequently "zoned out," consistently acting like the class clown or disrupting class. (Humor is a great distraction from reality.) Even if you are wrong, you are letting children know that if they ever need to talk (common need), you're willing to listen.

CONSIDER ASKING PROBING QUESTIONS IF A CHILD EXHIBITS ANY OF THE FOLLOWING:

- Sudden and extreme changes in character or behaviors
- Excessive anger or sadness
- Isolating behaviors
- Acting out behaviors (bullying or class clown)

If you suspect a child is being abused it can be difficult to have these tough conversations. You may need to get children away from their peers or you may have to allow them to bring a peer with them. Either way, create an atmosphere of privacy and safety. This may mean spending quality time and making small talk. Then try the following:

- Tell them you've noticed some changes and that you are worried about them.

- Tell them you wanted to speak to them to see if they need any help.

- Reassure them they will not be in trouble for talking to you, that they have done nothing wrong, and that you are prepared to support them if something *is* wrong.

- If they disclose abuse, immediately seek professional help. Contact the appropriate authorities, including the police and child protective services.

As a former police officer, I'm aware that police and child welfare investigators are generally instructed not to ask leading questions. While this is intended to protect the integrity of an investigation and there is incredible value in that, it shouldn't be taken so far as to miss potential opportunities for actual disclosure. Keep in mind the research shows that children often need prompting. If a police officer or counselor strongly suspects abuse after investigating without asking probing questions, would it not be better to ask a few leading questions and stop the abuse from continuing, especially if the suspect still has access to children? The alternative of waiting for another unprompted disclosure in the future could put children at continued risk of abuse.

PART 6

A GLANCE AT THE BIGGER PICTURE OF ADULT MALE SEXUAL ABUSE

As the stories outlined in this research clearly indicate, sexual abuse can take place in any home or environment, regardless of a victim's age, ethnicity, faith or socioeconomic status. It happens to boys living in traditional nuclear families and single-parent households.

The focus of this book has been more heavily weighted toward the child victim, given the experiences of the men who participated in my research. The reality, however, is that sexual abuse is also common among adult men as well. It is just rarely spoken about. What follows are but a few examples of adult male sexual abuse as it is known to exist.

Research shows that male sexual abuse is common in the prison population. Men who are dominated and then raped in prison often are released in worse shape than when they went in. In prison, male rape tends to be more about exerting power and domination than about sexual pleasure.[174] Outside of prison, male rape is known to occur among men seeking same-sex relations. Common "hook up" techniques (not exclusively used among gay populations) may include attending certain parks or bars, or using social media or apps to meet others seeking sexual contact. These venues easily become hunting grounds for predators looking to offend. Men who hook up may agree to certain sexual activities but not others. Many are forced to engage in sexual activities they do not consent to. Men are also victimized by crimes involving date rape drugs commonly used on women.

Statistics taken in North America indicate that male sexual abuse occurs about half as frequently as female abuse. With approximately one out of every six males being victimized and approximately 17 million males in Canada, that's just shy of three million potential male victims in Canada alone.

Male abuse also happens globally. In countries like Cambodia, Thailand, the Philippines, and Vietnam, young boys are prostituted and even sold. Others are made to dress like girls and forced to perform sex acts for sex tourists who travel abroad for the sole purpose of exploiting children. This abuse may precede their later transition into "careers" as "ladyboys" (men who dress like women and perform, dance and so forth for tourists).

Men also become victims of sexual violence committed as an act of war. In countries such as Syria, Rwanda, Sudan, and the Democratic Republic of Congo, men, women and children are frequently forced to leave their homes due to political unrest or threats of violence. What happens to the men on their journeys toward safety is barely imaginable.[175] Men are commonly abducted and raped. Yet because it is denied by both the perpetrator and the victim, most people remain unaware that sexual abuse is commonly perpetrated by men against men as an act of war and as a means to annihilate their culture.[176]

Dr. Chris Dolan, the founder of The Refugee Law Project in Africa, studied the rape of men in Uganda. He spoke to displaced men who admitted they had been captured, raped, and survived being tortured by rebels, militants or soldiers of the Lord's Resistance Army.[177] The men reported that the entire time (weeks, months, even years) they were held captive, they were brutally, violently and repeatedly raped.[178] In the end, they were either set free or they escaped, often after being left for dead. Many were left with serious internal injuries, including anal bleeding. Others who had endured the same, succumbed to their injuries and were never found.

Some who survive return to their home communities but remain silent out of fear of being ostracized or prosecuted since homosexuality is a crime punishable by death in many African countries. Even someone suspected of engaging in homosexual acts can be imprisoned or killed. Others make their way to internal displacement camps and seek emergency relief and assistance. Although no formal statistics exist to indicate how many people have made this journey seeking asylum, Dr. Dolan stated that all of the male survivors he spoke to indicate that the numbers are staggering.

While rape of any type is horrific, rape as an act of war has many distinguishing features, including its severity and frequency.[179] Rape committed against men by men as an act of war is not a sexual act but an act of domination intended to humiliate, disempower, break apart families, and annihilate communities.

In other countries male sexual abuse is reported to occur within the military ranks. Former Canadian soldiers returning from Afghanistan report that young Afghan men join the Afghan National Army as a means to support their families. The smaller men are treated "like women" by higher-ranking officials, who are reported to state, "Boys are for pleasure; women are for babies." Smaller boys not in the army are also often marked with orange dots on their hands to indicate that they are "spoken for." Many of these young men beg the allied soldiers to assist them. Unfortunately, the soldiers have been ordered not to intervene and are powerless to help them. They see the bodies of those who jump to their death instead of being abused, then return home haunted by the images and pleas of those they have been unable to help.[180]

In 1867 the Canadian government instituted a policy of Aboriginal assimilation which was designed to transform communities from "savage" to "civilized."[181] Government agents took children from their homes and forced them to live in church-run residential schools. A large number of boys and girls sent to these schools endured malnutrition, neglect and physical, emotional and sexual abuse at the hands of those who ran the schools. (Remember pedophiles will do anything to get access to their victims. Many train to become spiritual leaders and assume roles that will grant them access to children.)

The abuse that took place in these church-run residential schools harmed an entire generation of Indigenous children and eroded their cultures.

Sadly, in the aftermath there are reports that a disproportionate number of victims-turned-offenders have emerged. Interviews conducted in some of Canada's northernmost Indigenous communities have revealed a shockingly high prevalence of sexual abuse. A large number of males who attended residential schools are now living among the 40 plus population in Canada. When abuse is perpetrated by someone associated with a person's faith, it is particularly damaging (referred to as sanctuary abuse) since it may also impact their ability to have faith.

Spiritual Damage

As a Christian myself I couldn't help but notice how many of the men I interviewed had been abused by someone associated with a Christian church. Naturally, I wondered how this had impacted their faith. When I asked Phillip, who was abused by his father, a Methodist minister, about his faith he said he no longer had a faith. "I am atheist." Aaron, who was abused by men associated with the Catholic Church, no longer wanted anything to do with religion. "What I needed was a true church."

After his abuse, Leonard questioned how a loving God could allow abuse to happen to him, a devoted Christian. So did a few of the others. It is not uncommon for people to question or lose their faith after being abused by someone claiming to be a follower of Christ. Many ask, "How could God 'allow' their abuse to happen?" "Why did God let my abuser get away with it?" and "Does God expect me to forgive them?" I will attempt to address these questions using the Bible as my source of reference.

The information provided below is by no means a full answer to these questions, nor is it intended to offend non-Christian readers. It is a brief look at what the Bible says to Christ followers. It is written in response to the tough questions posed above, because many believers need these issues to be reconciled.

How could God allow abuse to happen?

If you're a victim, know that the abuse and suffering you experienced was not God's will. What happened to you was actually of great offense to Him, and He is deeply grieved about it. Although in this world we are subject to suffering caused by the "free will" acts of others, God desires to heal you.

This concept may not be easy to understand since there seems to be a disconnect between God's goodness and human suffering. However, suffering can be understood only if you understand evil. Evil doesn't come from God. God did not create evil. In this world, God allows man to have free will. God's nature is love, and He loves to heal. He wants people to turn to Him out of their own free choice, but He never forces anyone to follow Him. Man has free will, and he often chooses evil.

One of the many promises found in His Word is that *if* we choose to walk in His ways, He will use "all things to work together for the good" (Romans 8:28 NJKV). This means that He will bring good out of all the bad things that happened to you if you let Him. I know this may be a difficult concept and that you may be thinking that no good could ever come out of being sexually abused. Yes, I get that. God is not saying it was good that you were abused. What He is saying, is that *if* you enter into a relationship with Him, He will use even the horrible things that happened to bring healing and restoration to you. He is promising that if you choose to follow Him, He will use it to bring you closer to Him. When we are closer, good things will begin to happen, things like healing and deliverance from sorrow and suffering.

Why did the abuser get away with it?

Those who question why God *allows* abuse to happen also wonder why their abusers seem to have *gotten away* with it. This also is a valid question, which again relies on an understanding of God and how He deals with sin. If you are a victim, know that God hates sin and injustice. Although the Bible states that He is "slow to anger and abounding in mercy" (Psalm 103:8 NKJV), God sees the big picture.

The Bible says that one day everyone will come before Him and "give an account" (Romans 14:12 NKJV) of themselves to Him. "He will render to every man according to his works" (Romans 2:5-6 AV), sending "tribulation and anguish on every soul of man who does evil" (Romans 2:9 NKJV), and "these will go away into everlasting punishment, but the righteous onto eternal life" (Matthew 25:46 NKJV). It also states, "Whoever causes one of these little ones who believe in Me to sin, it would be better for him if a millstone were hung around his neck, and he were drowned in the sea" (Mark 9:42 NKJV).

Since we are taught to believe that the true nature of God is love, perhaps one of the answers to why God doesn't eliminate offenders while they are in the act and why He "allows" abuse to continue is because of His desire to see them repent. He loves the sinner but not the sin, and desires that even those who commit the most heinous of acts change their ways and follow Christ. He is giving them a chance to repent, similar to how a parent may unconditionally love their own child, no matter how bad they are.

What about offenders?

Jesus never turned away a truly repentant heart. The Bible states, "There will be more joy in heaven over one sinner who repents than over 99 just persons who need no repentance" (Luke 15:7 NKJV). Jesus sat and ate with many significant sinners, healed them, and told them to change their ways and sin no more. Jesus was sent to heal those who are sick. "Those who are well do not need a physician, but those who are sick" (Luke 5:31 NKJV). As a victim, it may be helpful to think of your offender as someone who is sick and in need of help and healing, since healthy people don't commit sex crimes.

What about forgiveness?

Victims may also be reluctant to enter or remain in the Christian faith out of fear they will be expected to forgive their offenders. Although this again may be difficult to grasp, it is possible for two reasons. First, biblical forgiveness doesn't adhere to the old cliché of "forgive and forget." It doesn't ask you to forget the hurt and damage done by your abuser. Nor does it discount or minimize the suffering caused by your abuser. It also doesn't insist that you seek reconciliation with your offender. (In fact, doing so may be unsafe.) Biblical forgiveness means agreeing to surrender your abuser to the Lord, agreeing to stop seeking emotional or physical revenge, and letting Him deal with them.

"Beloved, do not avenge yourselves, but rather give place to wrath; for it is written, 'vengeance is Mine, I will repay,' says the Lord" (Romans 12:19 NKJV).

Biblical forgiveness is actually for you. It is meant to set you free. It isn't about your past but rather about your future.[182] Second, the Bible teaches that as you agree with God that you are willing to try this, God actually helps you succeed. This is what Jesus meant when He taught, "With men this is impossible, but with God all things are possible" (Matthew 19:26 NKJV). As you agree to cooperate God helps you. As you continue in the process He slowly (or quickly) sets you free from your bondage. He sets you free from your need and desire to seek your own vindication or justice. You could spend the rest of your life seeking it and never be successful. As you cooperate, God does for you what you could never do on your own. When you release your offender to Him, you are the one who is set free.

Please don't interpret this to mean that I believe if you have faith and can easily forgive that you don't also need to see a trained trauma therapist. God uses people to do His work.

Joyce Meyer, a popular Christian minister, is open about the fact that she was sexually abused by her father for years. On her TV program, *Enjoying Everyday Life,* she tells her story of how becoming a follower of Christ transformed her life. She now uses her history of pain and suffering to lead others in their own personal journey toward healing. She builds churches, wells, and feeding stations in impoverished nations. She even has a prison ministry. She is healed and she has truly walked the walk. Several of the men who participated in my research verbalized that the reason they were participating in my research was because they, too, wanted to use their pain to help others heal.

Two Testimonies of Healing

Leon shared his experience of Godly transformation.

"I drove drunk, I mean thousands of times over the years. Had I not gotten the second DWI [driving while intoxicated] charge, I may not be alive. I could be in jail. I could have killed somebody. That's the irony and where the cross comes in," he said. "I have to be really grateful. I am blessed. I lost my job, lost my house to foreclosure, and had to declare bankruptcy, but my experience with the Lord has been transformative. The things that I have gained—my life changed dramatically."

"I gained a tremendous freedom that has no price tag," added Leon. "I have gained a relationship with my four children and my wife that is stronger than ever because of the honesty and transparency of what I have gone through. There is this inner freedom. There's a very deep element of the cross in this. It was like coming up from darkness into light, like recapturing my innocence."

Michael shared his experience too. On New Year's Eve, the night Michael's wife left him, all the liquor stores were open, but he knew alcohol was not the answer and didn't drink a drop.

"The next day, I turned my life over to God. I was broken. I didn't know where else to go. But God can do amazing things when you actually acknowledge and talk about things. I spent a lot of time with the Bible, and I've had these amazing revelations come out of it. It wasn't a fluke."

Michael now understands that he is not defined by what happened to him. He said that being "open, honest, intimate and vulnerable" has helped him to not care so much about what others think of him.

"Now, it really doesn't matter. It's my story, and I've got to tell it because it can help me to be vulnerable and to be emotional in ways I've never been in my life. I think it's incredibly beneficial to be vulnerable. I want to do anything and everything I can to tell my story, not to be ashamed or embarrassed of it. I know I can help other people. It is so helpful to be with other people where you can talk about things and to actually talk about it and share my feelings, and realize I'm loved and accepted and to bring them into the light. God can heal."

In the words of Pastor Robert Morris of Gateway Church in Texas:

"This isn't weird, folks. It's good news."

CONCLUSION

I trust that after reading this book you have an increased awareness about the fact that male sexual abuse occurs far more commonly than previously recognized. It just isn't talked about enough. Many reasons for males' nondisclosure have now been identified through research. Now that you are aware of the significant physical, emotional, cognitive, and cultural barriers boys and men face when considering disclosing, combined with what we know about the body's response to trauma, it isn't hard to understand why male sexual abuse is a hidden epidemic. This has to change. Boys and men need support too. They need support to become all that they were created to become.

If you are a male survivor I hope you learned something valuable from this book. I also hope that you found the information both healing and helpful. I anticipate that after hearing the stories of other male survivors, you will have more clarity and feel validated in regard to your own abuse experience. I encourage you—call it what it is, abuse. Take the next step and seek support and find professional help. It is true what Aaron said:

"We have a voice now."

If you are a parent, teacher, or helping professional, this book was not meant to frighten you into sheltering the children in your life unnecessarily. I also don't want you to live in fear of allowing children to have older friends and relationships with their extended siblings, mentors, or coaches. Nor do I want you to stop them from engaging in sports, taking healthy risks, or enjoying the many activities still considered rites of passage into manhood. This book was not meant to cause you to suspect sexual abuse every time a child acts weird, isolates, or has a meltdown. But if these behaviors become a pattern, or your child begins to behave in ways that are significantly outside of their normal character, pay attention.

If you are a parent, make informed decisions. Educate your children about sexual abuse. If you now suspect grooming or abuse, I encourage you to follow your instincts and take action! You have a new level of awareness that is based on academic research. If you feel uneasy about asking questions, get support and trust that others will be willing to help too.

Boys and men who feel uneasy about seeking help are left to deal with trauma in the only ways they know how. They bury it, resort to using alcohol, drugs, and promiscuity, turn to violence, or commit suicide. Suicide is the second-highest cause of death among youth and young adults ages 15 to 34 in Canada, and the rate is higher among boys and men than girls and women. There are likely reasons why, and this has to change. Our boys and men depend on it.

As a society, we need to make more room for abused boys and men to come forward. We need to advertise that we will support them, begin to have the tough conversations, and remove the stigma. If you are a helping professional, I encourage you to engage in more conversations about male sexual abuse. Open the dialogue with your colleagues and the clients you serve. Remember men don't commonly discuss things they don't hear others discussing.

Finally, if you are a helping professional and you learned from this book, share it, pass it on, tell your clients about it, buy copies for your colleagues or at least tell them about it. We all need to do our part to create acceptance and awareness. Parents and professionals both need to become more aware of the prevalence and grooming tactics of perpetrators and prevent male sexual abuse from happening in future generations. On behalf of myself and the men who told their stories, thank you for taking the time to read this book.

APPENDIX

What to Do if Someone Discloses Abuse: M.A.L.E.

Make time and space for them to privately discuss their abuse for as long as they need and as soon as possible. Pick your time and location carefully, away from anyone around whom they don't feel safe. Ensure they know that there are professionals who can help and encourage them to seek such professional help. Support organizations for male childhood sexual abuse survivors are listed on page 171. If the individual is a child, reassure them that you will help—and do it.

Ask for more information, and be careful about jumping to conclusions after partial disclosures. Ask how you can support them, and offer a few supportive words, like "I'm glad you told me" and "I'm sorry that happened."

Listen and let them know you believe them. Don't tell them to put it in their past, forget it, or get over it. People need to organize their thoughts, see your reaction, and process their emotions. Don't offer solutions. Listening is helping.

Expect that they may be confused about how they feel about their abuse and don't judge their thoughts or feelings. Sometimes negative or abusive attention is the only real attention a child receives, and parts of the relationship may have been what they needed at the time. Normalize and validate their thoughts and feelings as best you can.

10 Myths Male Survivors Should Not Believe

1. That you are alone or that no one will believe you.

2. That you are the only male who has ever been abused by a family member, teacher, pastor, police officer, fellow prisoner, and so on.

3. That you asked for it, invited it, or are responsible for it happening.

4. That having an erection or ejaculating means you consented or enjoyed being abused.

5. That even though you were young, you were mature enough to consent to the sexual behaviors.

6. That it was your job to fight harder or stop it.

7. That "real men" never turn sex down.

8. That you are to blame for the continuation of abuse.

9. That it's not okay to talk about your thoughts, emotions, or your abuse.

10. That your abuse determined your sexual orientation or "made" you gay.

If you question your sexuality after being abused, work with a therapist trained in trauma and sexuality. They may be able to help you understand your innate desires.

You're an Abuse Survivor. How Do You Know if You Need Help?

1. Are you avoiding deep conversations, certain topics, places, or people?

2. Do you find yourself unable to engage in intimate relationships?

3. Are you isolating?

4. Do you feel like talking about it would make you cry?

5. Are you easily irritated or do you experience excessive anger, anxiety, or depression?

If you answered yes to any of these questions, find a trained therapist to assist you.

10 Things You Can Do for Yourself if You Are a Male Survivor

1. Talk about your abuse with people you trust.

2. Force yourself to socialize. Isolation creates its own problems.

3. Take care of your physical needs. Eat well, get proper sleep, exercise, and drink plenty of water.

4. Get treatment. Find a counselor or psychologist who specializes in working with male survivors. Consider attending a weekend of recovery event.

5. Learn about the body's response to trauma. Knowledge is power.

6. Learn more about attachment issues so you can stop harmful patterns, challenge your current ways of thinking, and avoid toxic relationships.

7. Join a men's group, and ask for and accept support from friends and family.

8. Stop believing the myths around abuse. Stop taking responsibility for something that isn't your fault.

9. Help someone else, even in small ways. Being kind to others releases positive endorphins and serotonin, which make us feel happier!

10. Access your faith.

Support Organizations

Organizations that provide services exclusively for male survivors exist throughout Canada and the United States, though they are not widely known. Valuable resources that can be accessed online include the following:

- The Men's Project in Ottawa, Ontario (https://menandhealing.ca/)

- The British Columbia Society For Male Survivors of Sexual Abuse in Vancouver (https://bc-malesurvivors.com/)

- Male Survivor in Long Valley, New Jersey (https://malesurvivor.org/)

- 1in6 in Los Angeles, California (https://1in6.org/)

Recommended Books

The resources listed here are meant to assist and support you. Some of them were discussed in this book. I neither sought nor received any financial support from any of these authors.

Adams, Kenneth M. *Silently Seduced: When Parents Make Their Children Partners.* Health Communications Inc., 2011.

Adams, Kenneth, and Alexander Morgan. *When He's Married to Mom: How to Help Mother-Enmeshed Men Open Their Hearts to True Love and Commitment.* Fireside, 2007.

Brown, Brené. *Daring Greatly: How the Courage to Be Vulnerable Transforms the Way We Live, Love, Parent, and Lead.* Avery, 2012.

Clinton, Tim, and Gary Sibcy. *Attachment: Why You Love, Feel, and Act the Way You Do.* Thomas Nelson, 2009.

Cloud, Henry, and John Townsend. *Boundaries: When to Say Yes, How to Say No to Take Control of Your Life.* Zondervan, 2017.

Fradkin, Howard. *Joining Forces: Empowering Male Survivors to Thrive.* Hay House UK Ltd, 2012.

Heffernan, Margaret. *Willful Blindness: Why We Ignore the Obvious at Our Peril.* Bloomsbury USA, 2012.

Levine, Amir, and Rachel S. F. Heller. *Attached: The New Science of Adult Attachment and How It Help You Find—And Keep—Love.* Tarcher Perigee (Penguin Books), 2012.

Lew, Mike. *Victims No Longer: The Classic Guide for Men Recovering from Sexual Child Abuse.* Harper Perennial, 2004.

ACKNOWLEDGMENTS

I would like to thank the men who shared the intimate details of their abuse experiences with me. I am honored that you trusted me to relay your stories accurately, and I recognize the courage it took. You inspired and motivated me to conduct this research and publish this book. I wish you continued healing and many blessings. I'd also like to thank my former supervisors, colleagues, and friends who supported, advised, and encouraged me.

ABOUT THE AUTHOR

Dr. Kelli Palfy began her professional career working in adult and youth corrections. Here she noticed a disproportionate number of males in the system. In 1996, she became an RCMP (Royal Canadian Mounted Police) officer, she took an interest in investigating sex crimes and went on to specialize in sex crimes committed against children internationally. Here, as she combed through video evidence, she witnessed first-hand the grooming tactics commonly used by sophisticated pedophiles.

After retiring from the RCMP, Dr. Palfy obtained her Ph.D. in Counseling Psychology from the University of Alberta. She conducted her doctoral research on the reasons why males don't commonly disclose sexual abuse. She is now a trained trauma therapist and public speaker on the topic of male sexual abuse. Dr. Palfy currently runs a small private practice where she works with male survivors of abuse, first responders and couples using Emotion-Focused and Cognitive Behavioral Approach, plus Eye Movement Desensitization and Reprocessing (EMDR). Outside of her professional life she enjoys hiking, cycling, swimming, kayaking, paddle boarding, hanging out with friends and her pets.

Visit Dr. Palfy at peaksandvalleyspsychology.com or contact her at Mentoo2020unspoken@gmail.com.

ENDNOTES

1 David Lisak, Jim Hopper, and Pat Song, "Factors in the Cycle of Violence: Gender Rigidity and Emotional Constriction," *Journal of Traumatic Stress* 9, no. 4 (1996), https://doi.org/10.1002/jts.2490090405.

2 Shana Conroy and Adam Cotter, "Self-Reported Sexual Assault in Canada, 2014," Statistics Canada, 2017, https://www150.statcan.gc.ca/n1/pub/85-002-x/2017001/article/14842-eng.htm.

3 Sigrun Sigurdardottir, Sigridur Halldorsdottir, and Sóley S. Bender, "Deep and Almost Unbearable Suffering: Consequences of Childhood Sexual Abuse for Men's Health and Well-Being," *Scandinavian Journal of Caring Science* 26, no. 4 (2012): 694, https://doi.org/10.1111/j.1471-6712.2012.00981.x.

4 Jackson Katz, "Leading Change" (presentation for Alberta Council of Women's Shelters, Edmonton, Canada, January 2014).

5 Richard Gartner, "Relational Aftereffects in Manhood of Boyhood Sexual Abuse," *Journal of Contemporary Psychotherapy* 29, no. 4 (1999): 319–53, https://doi.org/10.1023/A:1022982806437; Ramona Alaggia and Graeme Millington, "Male Child Sexual Abuse: A Phenomenon of Betrayal," *Clinical Social Work Journal* 36, no. 3 (2008): 265–75, https://doi.org/10.1007/s10615-007-0144-y.

6 Herb Goldberg, *The Hazards of Being Male: Surviving the Myth of Masculine Privilege* (New York: New American Library, 1976).

7 Leslee Kassing, Denise Beesley, and Lisa Frey, "Gender Role Conflict, Homophobia, Age, and Education as Predictors of Male Rape Myth Acceptance," *Journal of Mental Health Counselling* 27, no. 4 (2005), https://doi.org/10.17744/mehc.27.4.9wfm24f52kqgav37; Mike Lew, *Victims No Longer: The Classic Guide for Men Recovering from Sexual Child Abuse* (New York: HarperCollins, 2004); Lynn Sorsoli, Maryam Kia-Keating, and Frances K. Grossman, "I Keep that Hush-Hush: Male Survivors of Sexual Abuse and the Challenges of Disclosure," *Journal of Counselling Psychology* 55, no. 3 (2008): 333–45, https://doi.org/10.1037%2F0022-0167.55.3.333.

8 American Psychological Association, Boys and Men Guidelines Group, *APA Guidelines for Psychological Practice with Boys and Men* (Washington, DC: APA Psychological Association, 2018), http://www.apa.org/about/policy/psychological-practice-boys-men-guidelines.pdf.

9 Alaggia and Millington, "Male Child Sexual Abuse."

10 Richard Gartner, "Sexual Victimization of Boys by Men: Meaning and Consequences," *Journal of Gay and Lesbian Psychotherapy* 3, no. 2 (2000): 1–33, https://doi.org/10.1300/J236v03n02_01.

11 Gartner, "Relational Aftereffects."

12 Mike Hartill, "The Sexual Abuse of Boys in Organized Male Sports," *Men and Masculinities* 12, no. 2 (2009): 236, https://doi.org/10.1177/1097184X07313361.

13 Michael Hartill, "Sexual Abuse of Boys."

14 Chris Doucette, "Theo Fleury Helped Change Society's View of Child Sex Abuse Victims," *Toronto Sun*, July 1, 2013, https://torontosun.com/2013/07/01/theo-fleury-helped-change-societys-view-of-child-sex-abuse/wcm/8533717c-326a-44b6-8ae2-81081f9756d7.

15 Sheldon Kennedy, *Why I Didn't Say Anything: The Sheldon Kennedy Story* (Toronto, Canada: Insomniac Press, 2006).

16 James Barrell and Sydney Jourard, "Being Honest with Persons We Like," *Journal of Individual Psychology* 32, no. 2 (1976): 185–93.

17 Roy Levin and Willy van Berlo, "Sexual Arousal and Orgasm in Subjects Who Experience Forced on Non-Consensual Sexual Stimulation – A Review," *Journal of Clinical Forensic Medicine* 11, no. 2 (2004): 82–88, https://doi.org/10.1016/j.jcfm.2003.10.008.

18 Stuart Turner, "Surviving Sexual Assault and Sexual Torture," in *Male Victims of Sexual Assault*, 2nd ed., edited by Gillian C. Mezey and Michael B. King (Oxford: Oxford University Press, 2000), 75–86.

19 Gillian Mezey and Michael King, *Male Victims of Sexual Assault*, 2nd ed. (New York: Oxford University Press, 2000).

20 Fuchs, "Male Sexual Assault."

21 Emily Nagoski, "The Truth About Unwanted Arousal," posted May 2018, TED video, 15:17, https://www.ted.com/talks/emily_nagoski_the_truth_about_unwanted_arousal.

22 A. J. Perez, "Ohio State Hit with Two Lawsuits over Sexual Abuse Allegations Made against Team Doctor," *USA Today*, July 17, 2018, https://www.usatoday.com/story/sports/college/2018/07/17/ohio-state-lawsuits-former-wrestlers-claim-university-officials-ignored-complaints/793916002.

23 Lisak, Hopper, and Song, "Factors in the Cycle of Violence."

24 Shanta R. Dube, Robert F. Anda, Charles L. Whitfield, David W. Brown, Vincent J. Felitti, Maxia Dong, and Wayne H. Giles, "Long-Term Consequences of Childhood Sexual Abuse by Gender of

Victim," *American Journal of Preventative Medicine* 28, no. 5 (2005), 430–38, https://doi.org/10.1016/j.amepre.2005.01.015.

25 Zoë Peterson, Emily Voller, Melissa Polunsy, and Maureen Murdoch, "Prevalence and Consequences of Adult Sexual Assault of Men: Review of Empirical Findings and State of the Literature," *Clinical Psychology Review* 31, no. 1 (2011): 102, https://doi.org/10.1016/j.cpr.2010.08.006.

26 Tiffany Artime, Ethan McCallum, and Zoë Peterson, "Men's Acknowledgement of Their Sexual Victimization Experiences," *Psychology of Men and Masculinity* 15, no. 3 (2014): 313–23, https://doi.org/10.1037/a0033376.

27 Conroy and Cotter, "Self-Reported Sexual Assault in Canada, 2014."

28 Patrick J. O'Leary and James Barber, "Gender Differences in Silencing Following Childhood Sexual Abuse," *Journal of Child Sexual Abuse* 17, no. 2 (2008): 133–43, https://doi.org/10.1080/10538710801916416.

29 Gene Abel, Judith Becker, Marty Mittelman, Jerry Cunningham-Rathner, Joanne Rouleau, and William Murphy, "Self-Reported Sex Crimes of Nonincarcerated Paraphiliacs," *Journal of Interpersonal Violence* 2, no. 1 (1987): 3–25, https://doi.org/10.1177/088626087002001001.

30 Abel et al., "Self-Reported Sex Crimes," 22.

31 Bill Watkins and Arnon Bentovim, "The Sexual Abuse of Male Children and Adolescents: A Review of Current Research," *Journal of Child Psychology and Psychiatry* 33, no. 1 (1992): 197–248, https://doi.org/10.1111/j.1469-7610.1992.tb00862.

32 Anthony Baker and Sylvia Duncan, "Child Sexual Abuse: A Study of Prevalence in Great Britain," *Child Abuse and Neglect* 9 (1985): 457–67, https://doi.org/10.1016/0145-2134(85)90054-7.

33 Clayton M. Bullock and Mace Beckson, "Male Victims of Sexual Assault: Phenomenology, Psychology, Physiology," *Journal of the American Academy of Psychiatry and the Law Online* 39, no. 2 (2001): 197–205.

34 Susan McDonald and Adamira Tijerino, *Male Survivors of Sexual Abuse and Assault: Their Experiences* (Ottawa, Canada: Department of Justice Canada, 2013), http://www.justice.gc.ca/eng/rp-pr/cj-jp/victim/rr13_8/rr13_8.pdf.

35 Matt Logan, "Wolves in Sheep's Clothing: Most Child Molesters Blend into the Background," *HALO Forensic Behavioural Specialists* (blog), February 22, 2010, https://mloganhalo.blogspot.com/2010/02/wolves-in-sheeps-clothing-most-child.html.

36 Logan, "Wolves in Sheep's Clothing."

37 Gene Abel, Judith Becker, Marty Mittelman, Jerry Cunningham-Rathner, Joanne Rouleau, and William Murphy, "Self-Reported Sex Crimes of Nonincarcerated Paraphiliacs," *Journal of Interpersonal Violence* 2, no. 1 (1987): 3–25, https://doi.org/10.1177/088626087002001001; Logan, "Wolves in Sheep's Clothing."

38 Ian Nisbet, Peter Wilson, and Stephen Smallbone, "A Prospective Longitudinal Study of Sexual Recidivism among Adolescent Sex Offenders," *Sexual Abuse: A Journal of Research and Treatment* 16, no. 3 (2004): 223–34, https://doi.org/10.1177/2F107906320401600304.

39 Logan, "Wolves in Sheep's Clothing."

40 American Psychiatric Association, *Diagnostic and Statistical Manual of Mental Disorders*, 5th ed. (Washington, DC: American Psychiatric Association, 2013).

41 American Psychiatric Association, *Diagnostic and Statistical Manual of Mental Disorders*, 5th ed., 699.

42 Logan, "Wolves in Sheep's Clothing."

43 Logan, "Wolves in Sheep's Clothing."

44 Logan, "Wolves in Sheep's Clothing."

45 Lanning, *Child Molesters: A Behavioral Analysis for Professionals Investigating the Sexual Exploitation of Children* (Alexandria, VA: National Center for Missing and Exploited Children, 2010)

46 Lanning, *Child Molesters*, 27.

47 Lanning, *Child Molesters*.

48 Joe Sullivan and Anthony Beech, "Professional Perpetrators: Sex Abusers Who Use Their Employment to Target and Sexually Abuse the Children with Whom They Work," *Child Abuse Review* 11 (2002), https://doi.org/10.1002/car.737.

49 Lanning, *Child Molesters*, 27.

50 Matthew Colton, Susan Roberts, and Maurice Vanstone, "Sexual Abuse by Men Who Work with Children," *Journal of Child Sexual Abuse* 19 (2010): 345–64, https://doi.org/10.1080/10538711003775824; Lanning, *Child Molesters*; Logan, "Wolves in Sheep's Clothing"; Joe Sullivan and Anthony Beech, "A Comparative Study of Demographic Data Relating to Intra- and Extra-Familial Child Sexual Abusers and Professional Perpetrators," *Journal of Sexual Aggression* 10, no. 1 (2004): 39–50, https://doi.org/10.1080/1355260041000166778.

51 Lanning, *Child Molesters*.

52 Logan, "Wolves in Sheep's Clothing."

53 Logan, "Wolves in Sheep's Clothing."

54 Sullivan and Beech, "A Comparative Study of Demographic Data."

55 Logan, "Wolves in Sheep's Clothing."

56 Ramona Alaggia and Graeme Millington, "Male Child Sexual Abuse: A Phenomenon of Betrayal," *Clinical Social Work Journal* 36, no. 3 (2008): 265–75, https://doi.org/10.1007/s10615-007-0144-y; Karen J. Terry and Joshua D. Freilich, "Understanding Child Sexual Abuse by Catholic Priests from a Situational Perspective," *Journal of Child Sexual Abuse* 21, no. 4 (2012): 437–55, https://doi.org/10.1080/10538712.2012.693579.

57 Logan, "Wolves in Sheep's Clothing."

58 Jacy Marmaduke, "'Pedophile Hunter' Mom Travels to Mexico to Find Fugitive Accused of Molesting Her Son," *9news*, April 11, 2018, https://www.coloradoan.com/story/news/2018/04/11/andrew-vanderwal-lydia-lerma-fort-collins-mexico-child-abuse/505163002/.

59 Lanning, *Child Molesters*.

60 Vanessa Miller, "Matthew Sandusky, Adopted Son of Jerry Sandusky, in Cedar Rapids Will Share His Story of Abuse," *The Gazette*, May 6, 2019, https://www.thegazette.com/subject/news/matthew-sandusky-adopted-son-of-jerry-sandusky-will-share-his-story-of-abuse-in-cedar-rapids-20190506.

61 Logan, "Wolves in Sheep's Clothing."

62 Alaggia and Millington, "Male Child Sexual Abuse"; Terry and Freilich, "Understanding Child Sexual Abuse."

63 Lanning, *Child Molesters*.

64 Logan, "Wolves in Sheep's Clothing."

65 Lanning, *Child Molesters*.

66 Lanning, *Child Molesters*; Sullivan and Beech, "Professional Perpetrators."

67 Lanning, *Child Molesters*; Logan, "Wolves in Sheep's Clothing."

68 Logan, "Wolves in Sheep's Clothing"; Terry and Freilich, "Understanding Child Sexual Abuse."

69 This passage comes from a 2012 search warrant information template involving the paraphiliac, shared with me by Matt Logan, a retired RCMP officer who now works as a forensic behavioral specialist.

70 Logan, "Wolves in Sheep's Clothing."

71 Stuart Turner, "Surviving Sexual Assault and Sexual Torture," in *Male Victims of Sexual Assault*, 2nd ed., edited by Gillian C. Mezey and Michael B. King (Oxford: Oxford University Press, 2000), 75–86.

72 Matt Logan, "Wolves in Sheep's Clothing: Most Child Molesters Blend into the Background," *HALO Forensic Behavioural Specialists* (blog), February 22, 2010, https://mloganhalo.blogspot.com/2010/02/wolves-in-sheeps-clothing-most-child.html.

73 Richard B. Gartner, "Relational Aftereffects in Manhood of Boyhood Sexual Abuse," *Journal of Contemporary Psychotherapy* 29, no. 4 (1999): 319–53, https://doi.org/10.1023/A:1022982806437.

74 Gartner, "Relational Aftereffects"; Richard Gartner, "Cinematic Depictions of Boyhood Sexual Victimization," *Gender and Psychoanalysis* 4 (2000): 253–89 (2000); Lynn Sorsoli, Maryam Kia-Keating, and Frances K. Grossman, "I Keep that Hush-Hush: Male Survivors of Sexual Abuse and the Challenges of Disclosure," *Journal of Counselling Psychology* 55, no. 3 (2008): 333–45, https://doi.org/10.1037/0022-0167.55.3.333.

75 Gartner, "Relational Aftereffects"; Gartner, "Cinematic Depictions of Boyhood Sexual Victimization."

76 Gartner, "Cinematic Depictions of Boyhood Sexual Victimization."

77 Richard B. Gartner, "Sexual Victimization of Boys by Men: Meaning and Consequences," *Journal of Gay and Lesbian Psychotherapy* 3, no. 2 (2000): 1–33, https://doi.org/10.1300/J236v03n_01.

78 Gartner, "Relational Aftereffects"; Richard Gartner, "Cinematic Depictions of Boyhood Sexual Victimization," *Gender and Psychoanalysis* 4 (2000): 253–89, https://doi.org/10.1300/J236v03n02_01; Sorsoli, Kia-Keating, and Grossman, "I Keep that Hush-Hush."

79 Gartner, "Relational Aftereffects."

80 Gartner, "Relational Aftereffects."

81 Kenneth Lanning, *Child Molesters: A Behavioral Analysis for Professionals Investigating the Sexual Exploitation of Children* (Alexandria, VA: National Center for Missing and Exploited Children, 2010) 26.

82 Paola Valerio, "Who Let the Boys in? Discussion of an NHS Mixed Gender Group for Victims of Childhood Sexual Abuse," *British Journal of Psychotherapy* 27, no. 1 (2011): 79–92, https://doi.org/10.1111/j.1752-0118.2010.01223.x.

83 Howard Fradkin, *Joining Forces: Empowering Male Survivors to Thrive* (New York: Hay House, 2012); Lanning, *Child Molesters.*

84 Alaggia and Millington, "Male Child Sexual Abuse."

85 Eli Teram, Carol Stalker, Angela Hovey, Candice Schacter, and Gerri Lasiuk, "Towards Malecentric Communication: Sensitizing Health Professionals to the Realities of Male Childhood Sexual Abuse Survivors," *Issues in Mental Health Nursing* 27, no. 5 (2006), https://doi.org/10.1080/01612840600599994.

86 Fradkin, *Joining Forces.*

87 Bruce D. Perry and Maia Szalavitz, *The Boy Who Was Raised as a Dog and Other Stories from a Child Psychiatrist's Notebook: What Traumatized Children Can Teach Us About Loss, Love, and Healing* (New York: Basic Books, 2007).

88 Peter Levine and Maggie Kline, *Trauma Through a Child's Eyes: Awakening the Ordinary Miracle of Healing* (Berkeley, CA: North Atlantic Books, 2006); Babette Rothchild, *The Body Remembers: The Psychophysiology of Trauma and Trauma Treatment* (New York: Norton, 2000); Bessel van der Kolk, "The Complexity of Adaptation to Trauma Self-Regulation, Stimulus Discrimination, and Characterological Development," in *Traumatic Stress: The Effects of Overwhelming Experiences on Mind, Body and Society*, edited by Bessel van der Kolk, Alexander McFarlane, and Lars Weisaeth (New York: Guildford Press, 2007), 129–54.

89 Perry and Szalavitz, *Boy Who Was Raised as a Dog.*

90 Sandra Twardosz and John R. Lutzker, "Child Maltreatment and the Developing Brain: A Review of Neuroscience Perspectives," *Aggression and Violent Behavior* 15, no. 1 (2010): 59–68, http://doi.org/10.1016/j.avb.2009.08.003.

91 Allan Shore, "The Effects of Early Relational Trauma on Right Brain Development, Affect, Regulation, and Infant Mental Health," *Infant Mental Health Journal* 22, no. 1/2 (1996), 201–69; Bessel van der Kolk, "Neurobiology of Childhood Trauma and Abuse," *Child and Adolescent Psychiatric Clinics of North America* 12, no. 2 (2003): 293–317.

92 Rothchild, *The Body Remembers.*

93 van der Kolk, "Neurobiology of Childhood Trauma and Abuse."

94 van der Kolk, "Neurobiology of Childhood Trauma and Abuse."

95 Julie Rothbard and Phillip Shaver, Continuity of attachment across the life span. In Sperling Michael and Berman William (Eds). Attachment in adults. Clinical and developmental perspectives. (New York: Guilford Press, 1994).

96 Van der Kolk, 2003

97 Rothchild, *The Body Remembers*; Twardosz and Lutzker, "Child Maltreatment and the Developing Brain."

98 van der Kolk, van der Hart, and Marmar, "Dissociation and Information Processing."

99 American Psychiatric Association, *Diagnostic and Statistical Manual of Mental Disorder*s, 5th ed. (Washington, DC: American Psychiatric Association, 2013).

100 Levine and Kline, *Trauma through a Child's Eyes*; Rothchild, *The Body Remembers*; van der Kolk, "Complexity of Adaptation"; Bessel van der Kolk, "The Trauma Spectrum: The Interaction of Biological and Social Events in the Genesis of the Trauma Response," *Journal of Traumatic Stress* 1 (1988), 273–90; van der Kolk, van der Hart, and Marmar, "Dissociation and Information Processing."

101 van der Kolk, van der Hart, and Marmar, "Dissociation and Information Processing."

102 Richard M. Wenzlaff and Daniel M. Wegner, "Thought Suppression," *Annual Review of Psychology* 51 (2000): 59–91, https://doi.org/10.1146/annurev.psych.51.1.59.

103 Rothchild, *The Body Remembers*.

104 Candice Feiring, Lynn Taska, and Michael Lewis, "Adjustment Following Sexual Abuse Discovery: The Role of Shame and Attribution Style," *Developmental Psychology* 38, no. 1 (2002): 79–92, https://doi.org/10.1037//0012-1649.38.1.79.

105 Marcela Matos, José Pinto-Gouveia, and Vânia Costa, "Understanding the Importance of Attachment in Shame Traumatic Memory Regulation to Depression: The Impact of Emotion Regulation Process," *Child Psychology and Psychotherapy* 20, no. 2 (2013): 149–65, https://doi.org/10.1002/cpp.786.

106 Brené Brown, "Listening to Shame," posted March 2012, TED video, 20:32, https://www.ted.com/talks/brene_brown_listening_to_shame.

107 Brown, "Listening to Shame."

108 Gershon Kaufman and Lev Raphael, *Coming Out of Shame: Transforming Gay and Lesbian Lives* (Toronto, Canada: Penguin Random House, 1996), 10.

109 Kaufman and Raphael, *Coming Out of Shame*.

110 Brown, "Listening to Shame."

111 Brown, "Listening to Shame."

112 Ian Nisbet, Peter Wilson, and Stephen Smallbone, "A Prospective Longitudinal Study of Sexual Recidivism among Adolescent Sex Offenders," Sexual Abuse: A Journal of Research and Treatment 16, no. 3 (2004): 223–34, https://doi.org/10.1177/2F107906320401600304.

113 Lanning, *Child Molesters*.

114 Maria Nasjleti, "Suffering in Silence: The Male Incest Victim," *Child Welfare* 59, no. 5 (1980): 271.

115 Ramona Alaggia, "Disclosing the Trauma of Child Sexual Abuse: A Gender Analysis," *Journal of Loss and Trauma* 10, no. 5 (2005): 453–70, https://doi.org/10.1080/15325020500193895.

116 Lynn Sorsoli, Maryam Kia-Keating, and Frances K. Grossman, "I Keep that Hush-Hush: Male Survivors of Sexual Abuse and the Challenges of Disclosure," *Journal of Counselling Psychology* 55, no. 3 (2008): 339, https://doi.org/10.1037/0022-0167.55.3.333.

117 Sorsoli, Kia-Keating, and Grossman, "I Keep that Hush-Hush," 343.

118 Sorsoli, Kia-Keating, and Grossman, "I Keep that Hush-Hush," 341.

119 Michael E. Addis and James R. Mahalik, "Men, Masculinity, and the Contexts of Seeking Help," *American Psychologist* 58, no. 1 (2003): 5–14, https://doi.org/10.1037/0003-066X.58.1.5; Jennifer M. Lane and Michael E. Addis, "Male Gender Role Conflict and Patterns of Help Seeking in Costa Rica and the United States," *Psychology of Men and Masculinity* 6, no. 3 (2005): 155–68, https://doi.org/10.1037/1524-9220.6.3.155.

120 William Holmes and Gail Slap, "Sexual Abuse of Boys: Definition, Prevalence, Correlates, Sequelae, and Management," *Journal of American Medical Association* 280 (1998): 1855–62; Guy Holmes and Liz Offen, "Clinicians' Hypotheses Regarding Clients' Problems: Are They Less Likely to Hypothesize Sexual Abuse in Male Compared to Female Clients," *Child Abuse and Neglect* 20, no. 6 (1996): 493–501, https://doi.org/10.1016/0145-2134(96)00031-2.

121 Holmes and Offen, "Clinicians' Hypotheses Regarding Clients' Problems."

122 Alaggia, "Disclosing the Trauma of Child Sexual Abuse."

123 Alaggia, "Disclosing the Trauma of Child Sexual Abuse."

124 Julia Omarzu, "A Disclosure Decision Model: Determining How and When Individuals Will Self-Disclose," *Personality and Social Psychology Review* 4, no. 2 (2000): 174–85, https://doi.org/10.1207/S15327957PSPR0402_05.

125 Elizabeth Leonard, "A Social Exchange Explanation for the Child Sexual Abuse Accommodation Syndrome," *Journal of Interpersonal Violence* 11, no. 1 (1996): 107–117, https://doi.org/10.1177/088626096011001008.

126 Sally V. Hunter, "Disclosure of Child Sexual Abuse as a Life-Long Process: Implications for Health Professionals," *The Australian and New Zealand Journal of Family Therapy* 32, no. 2 (2011): 159–72, https://doi.org/10.1375/anft.32.2.159.

127 Tine K. Jensen, Wenke Gulbrandsen, Svein Mossige, Sissel Reichelt, and Odd Arne Tjersland,

"Reporting Possible Sexual Abuse: A Qualitative Study on Children's Perspectives and the Context for Disclosure," *Child Abuse and Neglect* 29, no. 12 (2005): 1395–413, https://doi.org/10.1016/j.chiabu.2005.07.004.

128 Bessel van der Kolk, "The Complexity of Adaptation to Trauma Self-Regulation, Stimulus Discrimination, and Characterological Development," in *Traumatic Stress: The Effects of Overwhelming Experiences on Mind, Body and Society,* edited by Bessel van der Kolk, Alexander McFarlane, and Lars Weisaeth (New York: Guildford Press, 2007), 197.

129 van der Kolk, "Complexity of Adaptation."

130 van der Kolk, "Complexity of Adaptation."

131 Sigrum Sigurdardottir, Sigridur Halldorsdottir, and Sóley S. Bender, "Deep and Almost Unbearable Suffering: Consequences of Childhood Sexual Abuse for Men's Health and Well-Being," *Scandinavian Journal of Caring Science* 26, no. 4 (2012): 688–97, https://doi.org/10.1111/j.1471-6712.2012.00981.x.

132 Ramona Alaggia, "Disclosing the Trauma of Child Sexual Abuse: A Gender Analysis," *Journal of Loss and Trauma* 10, no. 5 (2005): 453–70, https://doi.org/10.1080/15325020500193895; Howard Fradkin, *Joining Forces: Empowering Male Survivors to Thrive* (New York: Hay House, 2012).

133 John Bowlby, "Developmental Psychiatry Comes of Age," *American Journal of Psychiatry* 145, no. 1 (1998): 1–10, https://doi.org/10.1176/ajp.145.1.1.

134 Mary D. Salter Ainsworth, Mary C. Blehar, Everett Waters, and Sally Wall, *Patterns of Attachment: A Psychological Study of Strange Situations* (Hilldale, NJ: Erlbaum, 1978).

135 Amir Levine and Rachel Heller, *Attached: The New Science of Adult Attachment and How It Help You Find and Keep Love* (New York: Penguin Group, 2011).

136 Levine and Heller, *Attached.*

137 Levine and Heller, *Attached.*

138 Levine and Heller, *Attached.*

139 Tim Clinton and Gary Sibcy, *Attachment: Why You Love, Feel, and Act the Way You Do* (Brentwood, TN: Nelson, 2002).

140 Clinton and Sibcy, *Attachment*.

141 Leanne Campbell, David Fairweather, and Gail Palmer, "EFT Core Skills Training," workshop in Edmonton, Alberta, 2019.

142 Bessel van der Kolk and Alexander McFarlane, "The Black Hole of Trauma," in *Traumatic Stress: The Effects of Overwhelming Experiences on Mind, Body and Society*, edited by Bessel van der Kolk, Alexander McFarlane, and Lars Weisaeth (New York: Guildford Press, 2007), 4.

143 Babette Rothchild, *The Body Remembers: The Psychophysiology of Trauma and Trauma Treatment* (New York: Norton, 2000); Bessel van der Kolk, Onno van der Hart, and Charles Marmar, "Dissociation and Information Processing in Post-Traumatic Stress Disorder," in *Traumatic Stress: The Effects of Overwhelming Experiences on Mind, Body, and Society*, edited by Bessel van der Kolk, Alexander McFarlane, and Lars Weisaeth (New York: The Guildford Press, 2007).

144 Rothchild, *The Body Remembers*.

145 Rothchild, *The Body Remembers*; van der Kolk, van der Hart, and Marmar, "Dissociation and Information Processing."

146 Rothchild, *The Body Remembers*; van der Kolk, van der Hart, and Marmar, "Dissociation and Information Processing."

147 Bruce D. Perry and Maia Szalavitz, *The Boy Who Was Raised as a Dog and Other Stories from a Child Psychiatrist's Notebook: What Traumatized Children Can Teach Us about Loss, Love, and Healing* (New York: Basic Books, 2007).

148 Peter Levine, *The Body as a Healer: Transforming Trauma and Anxiety* (Publisher: Lyons, CO, 1992).

149 Rothchild, *The Body Remembers*; van der Kolk, van der Hart, and Marmar, "Dissociation and Information Processing."

150 van der Kolk, van der Hart, and Marmar, "Dissociation and Information Processing."

151 Rothchild, *The Body Remembers*.

152 Perry and Szalavitz, *Boy Who Was Raised as a Dog*.

153 Perry and Szalavitz, *Boy Who Was Raised as a Dog*.

154 Perry and Szalavitz, *Boy Who Was Raised as a Dog*.

155 Marcela Matos, José Pinto-Gouveia, and Vânia Costa, "Understanding the Importance of Attachment in Shame Traumatic Memory Regulation to Depression: The Impact of Emotion Regulation Process," *Child Psychology and Psychotherapy* 20, no. 2 (2013): 149–65, https://doi.org/10.1002/cpp.786.

156 Perry and Szalavitz, *Boy Who Was Raised as a Dog.*

157 Madhumita Murgia, "How Stress Affects Your Brain," posted November 9, 2015, YouTube video, 4:15, https://youtu.be/WuyPuH9ojCE.

158 van der Kolk, van der Hart, and Marmar, "Dissociation and Information Processing."

159 Jim Hopper, "Neuroscience, Mindfulness & Yoga for Transforming Trauma" (presentation at the Summer Institute on Men, Trauma and Change, The Men's Project, Ottawa, Canada, June 2012); Patrick O'Leary, Carol Coohey, and Scott D. Easton, "The Effect of Severe Child Sexual Abuse and Disclosure on Mental Health during Adulthood," *Journal of Child Sexual Abuse* 19, no. 3 (2010): 275–89, https://doi.org/10.1080/10538711003781251.

160 John Briere, Stacey Kaltman, and Bonnie L. Green, "Accumulated Childhood Trauma and Symptom Complexity," *Journal of Traumatic Stress* 21, no. 2 (2008): 223–26, https://doi.org/10.1002/jts.20317; Wendy D'Andrea, Bradley Stolbach, Julien Ford, Joseph Spinazzola, and Bessel Van der Kolk, "Understanding Interpersonal Trauma in Children: Why We Need a Developmentally Appropriate Trauma Diagnosis," *American Orthopsychiatric Association* 82, no. 2 (2012): 187–200, https://doi.org/10.1111/j.1939-0025.2012.01154.x.

161 D'Andrea et al., "Understanding Interpersonal Trauma in Children."

162 D'Andrea et al., "Understanding Interpersonal Trauma in Children."

163 Peter Levine and Maggie Kline, *Trauma Through a Child's Eyes: Awakening the Ordinary Miracle of Healing* (Berkeley, CA: North Atlantic Books, 2006).

164 Sigurdardottir, Halldorsdottir, and Bender, "Deep and Almost Unbearable Suffering."

165 van der Kolk, van der Hart, and Marmar, "Dissociation and Information Processing."

166 Fradkin, *Joining Forces.*

167 José Pinto-Gouveia and Marcela Matos, "Can Shame Memories Become a Key to Identity? The Centrality of Shame Memories Predicts Psychopathology," *Applied Cognitive Psychology* 25, no. 2 (2011): 281–90, https://doi.org/10.1002/acp.1689.

168 American Psychiatric Association, *Diagnostic and Statistical Manual of Mental Disorders*, 5th ed. (Washington, DC: American Psychiatric Association, 2013).

169 van der Kolk, van der Hart, and Marmar, "Dissociation and Information Processing."

170 Perry and Szalavitz, *Boy Who Was Raised as a Dog*.

171 Margaret Heffernan, *Willful Blindness: Why We Ignore the Obvious at Our Peril* (New York: Bloomsbury USA, 2012).

172 Robert Burton, *On Being Certain: Believing You Are Right Even When You Are Not* (New York: St. Martin's Press, 2008).

173 Sandy Kleven, *Talk about Touch* (Kirkland, WA: Illumination Arts Publishing, 2012).

174 Matt Logan, RCMP Behavioral Sciences Group Training and personal communication, 2004.

175 Refugee Law Project, *Gender against Men*, 2009, video, 43:43, https://www.refugeelawproject.org/component/allvideoshare/video/gender-against-men.

176 Will Storr, "The Rape of Men," *The Guardian*, July 17, 2011, https://www.theguardian.com/society/2011/jul/17/the-rape-of-men.

177 Storr, "Rape of Men."

178 Refugee Law Project, *Gender against Men*.

179 Kristine Hagen and Sophie Yohani, "The Nature and Psychosocial Consequences of War Rape for Individuals and Communities," *International Journal of Psychological Studies* 2, no. 2 (2010): 14–25, https://doi.org/10.5539/ijps.v2n2p14; Refugee Law Project, *Gender against Men*.

180 Two former Clients (former Canadian soldiers) described this to me in 2018.

181 Manitoba Trauma Informed Education and Resource Centre, "Residential Schools," accessed October 26, 2018, https://trauma-informed.ca/trauma-and-first-nations-people/residential-schools.

182 John Burns and Helen Burns, "Love, Sex and Marriage" (presentation at Break Forth One conference, Edmonton, Canada, January 2019).

Made in the USA
Middletown, DE
18 December 2022

19367744R00120